THE RECORDED SAYINGS OF
ZEN MASTER JOSHU

CHAO-CHOU CHAN-SHIH YU-LU

The Recorded Sayings of Zen Master Joshu

Translated and introduced by
James Green

With a foreword by Keido Fukushima Roshi

SHAMBHALA
Boston
2001

SHAMBHALA PUBLICATIONS, INC.
Horticultural Hall
300 Massachusetts Avenue
Boston, Massachusetts 02115
www.shambhala.com

Translation and introduction © 1998 by James Green

Published by arrangement with AltaMira Press, a division of Sage Publications, Inc.
1630 North Main St., Suite 367, Walnut Creek, CA 94596 U.S.A.
Explore@altamira.sagepub.com

For more information about the International Sacred Literature Trust, please
write to the ISLT at: 22 Northumberland Avenue, London WC2N 5AP, UK

Originally photoset in Sabon by Northern Phototypesetting
Company Limited, Bolton, UK
Printed in the United States of America

⊛ This edition is printed on acid-free paper that meets the American
National Standards Institute z39.48 Standard.
Distributed in the United States by Random House, Inc., and in
Canada by Random House of Canada Ltd

The Library of Congress catalogs the previous edition of this book as follows:
Chao-chou, Shih, 778–897
[Chao-chou ch'an shih yü lu. English]
The recorded sayings of Zen Master Joshu / translated by James Green
p.   cm.

ISBN-10: 1-57062-870-X
ISBN-13: 978-1-57062-870-2

1. Zen Buddhism—Early works to 1800.   1. Green, James   11. Title.
BQ9265.C4513 1998a
294.3'927—dc21
98-4303
CIP

INTERNATIONAL
SACRED
LITERATURE
TRUST

The International Sacred Literature Trust was established to promote understanding and open discussion between and within faiths and to give voice in today's world to the wisdom that speaks across time and traditions.

What resources do the sacred traditions of the world possess to respond to the great global threats of poverty, war, ecological disaster and spiritual despair?

Our starting-point is the sacred texts with their vision of a higher truth and their deep insights into the nature of humanity and the universe we inhabit. The translation programme is planned so that each faith community articulates its own teachings with the intention of enhancing its self-understanding as well as the understanding of those of other faiths and those of no faith.

The Trust particularly encourages faiths to make available texts which are needed in translation for their own communities and also texts which are little known outside the tradition but which have the power to inspire, console, enlighten and transform. These sources from the past become resources for the present and future when we make inspired use of them to guide us in shaping the contemporary world.

Our religious traditions are diverse but, as with the natural environment, we are discovering the global interdependence of human hearts and minds. The Trust invites all to participate in the modern experience of interfaith encounter and exchange which marks a new phase in the human quest to discover our full humanity.

Dedicated to Fukushima Roshi

Knowingly and purposefully the transgression was made.
Chao-chou (Joshu)

Contents

Foreword	xi
Acknowledgments	xiii
Introduction	xv
Translator's Note	xxv

THE RECORDED SAYINGS OF ZEN MASTER JOSHU

BIOGRAPHY	3
PART ONE: Lectures, Questions & Answers	11
PART TWO: Questions & Answers	77
PART THREE: Poems & Records from Pilgrimages	137
APPENDIX	176
Glossary	179

Foreword

The place of Chao-chou Ts'ung-shen, known in Japan and the West as "Joshu", is extremely important as well as unique in the history of Chinese Ch'an (Zen). Chao-chou (778–897 CE) and his contemporary Lin-chi I-hsuan (d. 867 CE) were the two great masters of "North-of-the-[Yellow]-River Zen" which flourished alongside "South-of-the-[Yangtze]-River Zen" during the T'ang dynasty.

Chao-chou's Zen character has been called "lip Zen". His verbal expression of Zen was so superb that light seemed to flow from his lips. This quality pervades his *Recorded Sayings*, but one of my favourite examples of it is his answer to a monk's question "What is the depth of the deep?":

"What depth of the deep should I talk about, the seven of seven or the eight of eight?" (see no. 38)

The answer shows the wonderful originality and freedom of his "light-emitting lips". This superb book, translated here in its entirety, is a record filled with Chao-chou's tremendous Zen activity, overflowing with the unique "great activity and great function" of mature T'ang dynasty Ch'an/Zen.

The translator, James Green, has been a disciple of mine since 1974 when he trained under me as a monk for eighteen months. He sat in *zazen* (sitting meditation) exceptionally well with perfect posture and was one of the best of my American disciples. During his stay in Japan, he showed great interest in *The Recorded Sayings of Zen Master Joshu*. In my view, Jim has in him something similar to Chao-chou/Joshu. I do not know whether or not he is aware of this but perhaps this is one reason for his fascination with *The Recorded Sayings*. He certainly has affinity with Zen monks of this style and respects and loves Chao-chou. I believe this was a source of strength in bringing to completion such a difficult translation.

It is now over twenty years since this translation was begun. The long-awaited publication of the English translation of the complete text is a source of great pleasure to me. Through this translation, I sincerely hope that many English-language readers will come to a deeper understanding of authentic "Patriarch Zen" as the Zen brought from India to China by Bodhidharma is called. I strongly recommend this English translation.

Keido Fukushima
Head Abbot of the Tofukuji branch of Rinzai Zen
Zen Master of the Tofukuji Training Monastery
Kyoto, August 1996

Acknowledgments

I wish to thank Hap Tivey and Tayo Gabler for their participation in rendering the text into English during our stay together at Hofuku-ji monastery; Hisashi Miura for continuing friendship and encouragement; and, of course, Fukushima Roshi, without whom this manuscript would not exist. A special thanks to Jeff Shore for his invaluable assistance, and to Naomi Rubine and San Albers for clerical and editorial help.

James Green

Our thanks as always to Quentin Smith and Doreen Mantle for their continued support, and to Alison Forbes and Wendy Clifford, both of whom worked on the administration of the book. Also to Martine Batchelor and Jeff Shore for making the links that made the publication of this book possible.

International Sacred Literature Trust

Introduction

In writing an introduction to *The Recorded Sayings of Zen Master Joshu* I would like to be as brief as possible, as the text speaks for itself. Yet, to assume an in-depth understanding of the history of Zen on the part of the reader would be a mistake. Therefore, let me provide a brief sketch of its context in history as background to the teachings contained in the text.

"Zen" is a Japanese name for a particular teaching tradition within the overall framework of Buddhism which came to Japan through China from India where it originated in the life of Gautama Buddha around 500 BCE.

Gautama was not born as "Buddha", that is "the enlightened one", in the sense that this was not an inherited title. Being Buddha was something he earned through spiritual exploration. His diligent spiritual quest brought him to what is traditionally called "enlightenment", a direct experience of the core reality of being wherein the apparent paradox of subject/object duality is resolved, and the underlying life force, which is both something and nothing at once, is perceived.

In the aftermath of his enlightenment experience, Gautama felt it was his duty to help others to the same experience and to enunciate his insight into the nature of human existence. Thus, he began to teach those who showed interest. The foundation of his teaching was that having a similar enlightenment would create a release from suffering and spiritual anxiety – a *nirvana*, a state of being free from this suffering and spiritual anxiety.

This basic teaching of Gautama and later doctrine of Buddhism is embodied in what are called the "Four Noble Truths": (1) life is suffering, (2) suffering arises from incessant desires, (3) there is a way to transcend being controlled by desire, (4) this way is the Eight-Fold Path.

The Eight-Fold Path taught by Gautama as the route to the desireless state of nirvana was:

1   right understanding
2   right mindfulness
3   right speech
4   right bodily conduct
5   right livelihood
6   right effort
7   right attentiveness
8   right concentration.

During his lifetime Gautama's fame grew and he attracted a large number of followers. In addition to the creation of a monastery or *ashram* where those who responded to his message came to live life according to his teachings, a body of written material began to accumulate. These scriptures or *sutras* became the doctrinal core of Buddhism as it began its voyage through cultural space and time across Asia and eventually Europe and the Americas.

The sutras comprise the teaching of Gautama as compiled by others, presumed to be his contemporaries or near-contemporaries. This scriptural heritage ensured the preservation of Gautama's teaching, yet, as time passed, particular sutras within the overall scriptural body became the focal points upon which sectarian differences evolved within Buddhism.

A discussion of the myriad divergencies within Buddhism would be quite lengthy and I have given this facet of Buddhist history mention only to emphasize the following point: in addition to there being various sects based on the scriptural tradition of Gautama's teaching, there is also said to be an oral tradition. The oral tradition is presumed to embody the direct personal teaching of Gautama to a select inner circle of disciples, and from them to successive generations of individuals who were then authorized to be the bearers of the oral tradition.

Buddhism became institutionalized as it endured through the centuries after Gautama's lifetime, and the sutras were copied and studied. Concurrently, the oral tradition was passed from master to disciple.

Around two hundred and fifty years after Gautama's death his teaching reached a socio-cultural climax in India with the ascendancy of the powerful King Ashoka, who reigned 274–236 BCE. Ashoka embraced Buddhism, established monasteries and financed missionaries to spread Buddhism to southern India, Sri Lanka and Kashmir in the north. The arrival of Buddhism in the northern regions facilitated access to the Eurasian trading routes to China. It is generally accepted that Buddhist missionaries had arrived in China by 100 CE but met limited acceptance in a society that was organized around the complementary teachings of Confucianism and Taoism.

For two hundred years Buddhist monks from India maintained a tenuous foothold in China and had little impact on the society other than a cumulative presence over time. This enduring presence gave them a certain legitimacy within China so that when the great Han dynasty collapsed during the third century CE the Buddhist teachings were available as a philosophical and spiritual alternative in the ensuing chaos and social instability that engulfed China for the next three hundred years. During this fractious "Warring States Period", China eventually divided into two nations – one in the south, which was a weak coalition of feudal states ruled by ethnic Chinese, and one in the north, ruled by non-Chinese from Central Asia.

The rulers of the Northern Kingdom found it to their advantage to displace the traditional Taoist/Confucian belief system with Buddhism as a means of imposing their own identity on the society. In the south the collapse of the old institutions and the flood of displaced people from the north led the intellectuals and the wealthy families to question the Confucian/Taoist mind-set and to be receptive to something new.

For their part, the Buddhists were able to use their more than two hundred years in China to express their teachings in a way that made them coherent to, and coalescent of, Confucianist/Taoist teachings. Consequently, Buddhism was embraced as a mainstream religion in China during this period.

Eventually the southern Chinese were able to ally themselves around a strong ruler and defeated the Northern Wei dynasty (c. 589 CE), leading to the establishment of the T'ang dynasty.

During the T'ang dynasty, China was arguably the most advanced civilization on the planet – "advanced" in the sense of a prolonged peace and prosperity creating a large middle class and therefore the time and inclination to develop the cultural, artistic and philosophical dimensions of human experience. One of the various sects of Buddhism to flourish at this time was the Ch'an (Japanese: Zen) sect.

Ch'an first appeared in China toward the end of the Northern Wei dynasty (440–589 CE) with the arrival of an Indian monk named Bodhidharma. It is documented in Ch'an/Zen literature that Bodhidharma's presence became known to the Emperor Wu when it was rumoured within the Buddhist community that a great master of the oral tradition had arrived from India in 527.

Subsequently, Emperor Wu, who was an ardent benefactor of Buddhism, invited Bodhidharma to his palace and asked him, "What merit do I have?" Bodhidharma answered, "Nothing". The emperor didn't understand and asked for an explanation. Bodhidharma said, "Vast emptiness, nothing sacred", and left.

Bodhidharma is held to be the "Twenty-eighth Patriarch" in the Ch'an/Zen tradition. That is, he is the twenty-eighth generation of holders of the oral teaching of Gautama. He is also considered to be the First Patriarch of Ch'an in China. Although Bodhidharma did not find favour with the imperial court in his lifetime, he did have followers and was able to perpetuate the oral tradition.

In the 100 to 150 years after Bodhidharma, the Ch'an teaching was passed from master to disciple. These early Ch'an masters were men who did not live at large temples, nor did they teach large numbers of disciples; Bodhidharma himself lived in a small hut in northern China near Luoyang (Japanese: Rakuyo) and, according to Zen history, sat facing the wall of a cliff behind his hermitage for nine years until Hui-k'o (Japanese: Eka), the Second Patriarch, came to learn from him. After receiving the Dharma (in Ch'an/Zen this refers to the acknowledgment from the master that the disciple's understanding is the same as his own), Hui-k'o taught in the streets throughout China until his death at the age of 107 in 593 CE. About the Third Patriarch, Seng-ts-an (Sosau), nothing is known, although he did leave behind one of the earliest of Ch'an writings, *Shin-jin mei (Trusting the Mind)*. The Fourth Patriarch, Tao-hsin (Doshin, 580–651 CE), was a hermit who lived in the mountains and left a small body of writings.

However, Hung-jen (Gunin), the successor of Tao-hsin, was able to assemble a large following and maintained a substantial temple as the T'ang era began to advance. By the end of Hung-jen's lifetime, Ch'an had become well known and, through his agency and that of his successor the Sixth Patriarch Hui-neng (Eno, d. 713), attained prominence in the Buddhist world. As well as Hui-neng, Hung-jen had many "descendants" who spread the teaching of Ch'an and erected many temples throughout China. Hui-neng himself had many worthy successors who actively taught Ch'an. Through the teaching of these masters, the possibility of awakening to the Dharma (the truth of the Buddha's teaching) through direct personal experience began to evoke a great deal of interest in the Chinese.

One of the factors that made Ch'an attractive to the Chinese was its central teaching that a direct experience of the truth of the Buddha's teaching is linked to a breakthrough realization which leads to nirvana, an "emptiness" of consciousness wherein the duality of subject/object is nullified, taking with it the constant traffic of desires. In the context of China this teaching resonated with the ancient Taoist teaching of "nothingness" and "non-doing". In addition, the notion of an oral or "secret" tradition was also familiar to the Chinese in the practice of traditional Taoism. Thus, with the begining of the great era of prosperity in the T'ang dynasty, Ch'an began to grow in popularity in China.

Two generations after Hui-neng (Eno), Ch'an came to fruition in two dynamic masters: Ma-tsu (Baso, 709–788) and Shih-t'ou (Sekito, 700–790). It was from the creativity and strength of expression of these two masters and their immediate successors that Ch'an was to reach its zenith in the latter years of the T'ang dynasty. During this time, from 750 to 900, most of the teachers revered in the Ch'an tradition lived and died: Tung-shan (Tozan), the originator of the present-day Soto Zen lineage, lived from 807 to 869; Lin-chi (Rinzai), the originator of the present-day Rinzai Zen lineage, lived from 810 to 866; Po-chang (Hyakujo) lived from 720 to 814; Yueh-shan (Yakusan) lived from 745 to 828; and Te-shan (Tokusan) lived from 785 to 865. It was at this time that Chao-chou (Joshu) also lived out his life.

The facts known about Chao-chou's life are few. He was born in 778 in the countryside of northern China and died in 897. After being initiated as a monk, he travelled to seek out his own teacher. At the age of eighteen, he met Nan-ch'uan (Nansen, 748–835), one of the most brilliant of the many successors of Ma-tsu, and eventually received the Dharma from him (see no. 1 of this book). After that he continued to reside at Nan-ch'uan's temple until the latter's death in 835 when Chao-chou was fifty-seven.

Following a three-year period of mourning, he started out on a pilgrimage throughout China saying, "Even if it is a boy of seven years, if he is better than me, I will ask for his teaching. Even if it is a man of a hundred years, if he is not as good as me, I will instruct him." Travelling for twenty years, he visited all the prominent Ch'an masters of his day and, finally, at the age of eighty, took up residence in a dilapidated temple in northern China. This was the Kuan-yin yuan (Kannon-In) in the province of Chao (Jo: Chao-chou/Joshu literally means "province of Chao/Jo"). He lived at Kuan-yin yuan for forty years, teaching the small number of monks who gathered around him, until his death at the age of 120. (In China, a person is one year old at birth.)

Chao-chou/Joshu was an enigmatic old man, twice as old as most

of the other "old men" (Ch'an masters) of the day, who had deep-
ened his own realization through personally lived experience, and
whose truth could be seen in his words and actions. Though Chao-
chou was one of the greatest Zen masters of the T'ang dynasty, his
personal line of "descendants" was weak and died out. One way of
accounting for this is to realize not only that the living conditions
of his temple were severe (cold winters and basic poverty) but also
that, by the end of his life, northern China was increasingly
engulfed in feudal warfare as the domnion of the T'ang emperor
weakened. Thus, the number of monks able to dwell in the north
of China (especially after 870) amidst such conditions was limited.

However, from another point of view, Chao-chou was a Ch'an
master of the old style and did not choose to become the master of
a large temple. Likewise, the few men who did try to carry out his
lineage may also have been people who were not eager to establish
themselves in large temples, but chose to live as fishermen and farm-
ers. (There were also frequent purges in Buddhism in China during
this period, particularly in 845.). However it may be, successors to
Chao-chou are not documented beyond two generations to around
the year 1000.

It was at this time, as China began to re-coalesce into a new unity
at the beginning of the Sung dynasty (960–1278), that Ch'an masters started to rely more and more on the Ch'an that had been vital
in the lives of their predecessors, the legendary masters of the T'ang
era. So it was that the written tradition of Ch'an became established. This written tradition consisted of collections of anecdotes
about the T'ang masters (as in the two texts mentioned below),
which were used as examples of, and as teaching tools with which
to evoke, the Ch'an (Zen) mind and catalyse the enlightenment
experience.

Thus, even though Chao-chou's personal line of descendants was
not in the mainstream of Sung dynasty Ch'an, it is a testament to
the power of his Ch'an that his teachings were preserved and utilized by later generations. In the waning stages of the Sung dynasty

(c. 1200), Buddhist pilgrims from Japan came in contact with Ch'an.

Although Buddhism had been introduced into Japan by Chinese missionaries in the sixth century, the teaching of the Ch'an sect was only finally brought back to Japan by Japanese Buddhists who, unsatisfied with the teachings available at home, took it upon themselves to venture to China seeking deeper teachings. Among these pilgrims were two eminent Japanese who founded strong lineages in Japan, Dogen and Eisai, in the twelfth century. Thus, it was the practice of Ch'an as it was conducted in the temples of the twelfth-century Sung dynasty that was the model they brought back and that is preserved in monastic Zen practice in Japan to this day.

This practice basically consists of a simple monastic life, long hours of meditation, personal dialogue with the master, and public lectures given by the master. In Japan today, especially within the Rinzai sect, both the personal dialogue with the master and the master's lectures are centred on anecdotes of Ch'an/Zen history as mentioned earlier. For those interested in the Zen mind and its portrayal in Zen literature, the *Recorded Sayings of Zen Master Joshu* is a shining jewel.

It is said of Chao-chou/Joshu that his "lips emitted light" because his manner of teaching was to speak words that profoundly expressed the Ch'an experience in a pithy and succinct manner. It is because of this spiritual dexterity that the teachings of Chao-chou/Joshu are the quintessential expression of the spiritual practice known as Ch'an/Zen. Though his life itself is an embodiment of the Zen ideal, it was his particular ability at Zen dialogue (*mondo*, lit. "question and answer") for which he is held so dear in the tradition. It is in the repartee of dialogue that the "Zen mind" of Joshu (as he is now more commonly known) is revealed and, for those who are curious about what the Zen mind may be, his dialogues provide a possible catalyst for insight.

In actual Zen spiritual practice, especially within the Rinzai Zen

tradition, the master will present the student with a particular anec-
dote (*koan*) from Zen history to reflect upon and to use as a start-
ing point for the student's own dialogue with the master directed
toward awakening the Zen mind. The impact of Joshu's presence
in the Zen tradition can be measured in the number of anecdotes
about him that are preserved in Ch'an/Zen literature and used as
teaching devices in this way in the Japanese Zen lineage.

In the two main collections of anecdotes that are used in the
Rinzai Zen lineage, the sayings of Joshu are numerous: of the forty-
eight anecdotes in the *Mumonkan* (Chinese: *Wu-men kuan*), five are
Joshu's. Among the one hundred anecdotes of the *Hekigan-roku*
(Chinese: *Pi-yen lu*), twelve are Joshu's sayings.

The copy of the *Recorded Sayings* that is translated here has a
preface by a priest of the Tsao-tung (Soto) sect of Zen, Yun-men
Yuan-chang (Unmon, 1565–1626). Yun-men attributes the compila-
tion of the text to Wen-yuan (Bun-en), one of the immediate disciples of Chao-chou. This attribution of the work to Wen-yuan is
probably based on the fact that he is mentioned many times in the
text. Modern scholars, however, doubt that Wen-yuan is responsi-
ble for compiling the text. The biography that precedes the three
parts of *The Recorded Sayings* was written by another immediate
disciple, Hui-ts'ung (Ezu), in the year 953, fifty-six years after the
death of Chao-chou. The text itself ends with a note that it was re-
edited by Ch'eng-shih (Choshoku), a monk of the Fa-yen (Hogen)
sect of Ch'an who was a contemporary of Hui-ts'ung. Thus, the
text was probably in circulation around the middle of the tenth century and certainly by the year 1000.

The text appeared in a collection of Ch'an teachings published
during the Sung and Yuan dynasties, *Ku-tsun-su yu-yau* (*The Essential Teachings of Ancient Masters*), published about 1267. The text
was also included in the *Zozokukyo* (Supplement to the Japanese
Edition of the Buddhist Canon), published about 1912.

This translation is from the Japanese translation edited and com-
mented upon by Professor Ryumin Akitsuki (*Joshu-roku*, Tokyo,

1972). Akitsuki's work on the text is greatly appreciated by this translator, as is the work of all the editors and transcribers of it through the centuries.

The work of translating the *Chao-chou Ch'an-shih Yu-lu* into English is undertaken from the standpoint that interest in Zen is growing in the West. In as much as the teachings of the past are the traditions of the present, those who come in contact with Zen in the West should have access to the forbears of the tradition from which the teachings of the people of today grow and upon which they rely. The text is, therefore, translated so as to be meaningful in ordinary English, rather than literal to the Chinese. It is ever a problem in translating to orient the direction of the translation so as to maintain a harmony between the "translated from" language and the "translated to" language.

In the case where the associations and secondary meanings of a language as rich as the Chinese language in general, and Zen language in particular, are being translated, explanatory notes are a necessity. However, the translation presented here contains explanatory notes only where there is a meaning in the Chinese which is not evident in the English words or where there is something understood in the Ch'an/Zen language that is not clear to Western readers. Also, where there are references to people, places and things that may be unknown to the reader, notes are provided. It is my hope that readers seeking elucidation of passages difficult to understand will take their questions to teachers and masters in the Zen tradition.

James Green

Translator's Note

The point of a translation is of course to take a text into another language, in this case English. Nevertheless, it is never possible to eradicate all "foreign" words, as sometimes they have no equivalents in the translated language or they are names. So although English is the language of this translation, three other languages, which reflect the migration of Buddhism from India to China, thence to Japan and finally to the West, also make an appearance.

Sanskrit, the ancient classical language of India, appears in the form of technical Buddhist/Eastern philosophical terms, for instance: Buddha, karma, Dharma and so on. Many of these now enjoy a currency in the English language and are not therefore italicized as "foreign words" but they are footnoted on first appearance and/or can be found in the glossary at the back of the book. Sanskrit words which have not been so widely absorbed in the West and which are given an English translation are italicized on first appearance.

Although this translation is from the Japanese edition and we have called it *The Recorded Sayings of Master Joshu* in deference to the more commonly known Japanese rendering of Joshu/Chaochou's name, he and the other monks referred to in this record were of course Chinese and known in their lifetime by Chinese names. I have chosen, therefore, to render the names of people, including that of Chao-chou (Joshu), as in the original Chinese but with the more commonly known Japanese pronunciation in brackets the first time it appears in a koan. Chinese place names are also given in this manner.

THE RECORDED SAYINGS OF
ZEN MASTER JOSHU

趙州眞際禪師語錄并行狀卷上

師即南泉門人也俗姓郝氏本曹州郝鄉人也諱從諗

鎭府有塔記云師得七百甲子歟值武王微沐避地岨崍

大食葷衣僧儀不易　師初隨本師行脚到南泉本師先

人事了師方久人事南泉在方丈內卧次見師來乃便問

近離什麼處師云瑞像院南泉云還見瑞像麼師云不見

即了見即如來南泉乃起問你見有主沙彌無主沙

弥師對云有主沙彌南泉云那箇是你主沙彌別處安

惟和尚尊體起居萬福南泉乃喚維那此沙彌別處安

排師受戒後聞受業師在曹州西住護國院乃歸院省覲

到後本師令郝氏云家之子遊方已迴其家親屬忻懌

一不往覲　來日流往觀焉所聞之乃云俗塵愛網無有了期

Biography

The master was a disciple of Nan-ch'uan (Nansen).[1] His family name was Ho (Kaku), and he was a native of Ho (Kaku) village in the province of Ts'ao (So).[2] His name as a monk was Ts'ung-shen (Jushin).

In the province of Chen (Chin)[3] there is a *stupa*,[4] the memorial of which reads:

> The Master attained the age of one hundred and twenty years. He was not shown any mercy by Emperor Wu[5] and was forced to flee to safe lands. He ate from trees, and made clothes from weeds. He did not take lightly the duties of a monk.

In the beginning the master went on pilgrimage, according to the directions of his original master,[6] and arrived at Nan-ch'uan's

---

[1] Nan-ch'uan P'u-yuan (Nansen Fugan) was a disciple of Ma-tsu Tao-i (Baso Doitsu). He was born in 748 and died in 835. His temple was in the province of Ch'ih (Chishu) in present-day Anhwei. Nan-ch'uan was one of the great masters of the T'ang dynasty.

[2] In present-day Shantung.

[3] The district in Chao province in northern China where Chao-chou's (Joshu's) temple was located. See note 10.

[4] A pagoda or other structure used to house the remains of the Buddha's body, but also for the remains of eminent priests.

[5] Emperor Wu started one of the three great persecutions of Buddhism in China in the years 841–846 CE.

[6] In Ch'an (Zen) a monk usually has two masters. One (the original master) initiates the boy as a novice monk (usually in his home district), and when the novice comes of age he goes on his own to seek a master under whom he can do Ch'an practice. The name of Chao-chou's original master is unknown.

place. With his original master, to be courteous was of utmost importance so the master was certainly courteous. While Nan-ch'uan was lying in his room, the master came to meet him. Seeing the master coming, Nan-ch'uan said, "Where have you come from?"

The master said, "From Shui-hsiang yuan."[7]

Nan-ch'uan said, "Then did you see the standing image [of the Buddha] there?"

The master said, "I don't see a standing image, I see a reclining Tathagata."[8]

Nan-ch'uan said, "Are you a novice with a master, or a novice without a master?"

The master said, "A novice with a master."

Nan-ch'uan said, "Where is your master?"

The master said, "In spite of the intense cold of early spring, I dare say your honourable body is enjoying good health."

Nan-ch'uan then called the head monk to him and said, "Give this novice a special seat [in the monks' hall]."

After the master received the commandments and ordination, he heard that his original master had moved to Hu-kuo yuan in the west of Ts'ao province,[9] so he returned there to pay his respects. Upon his return, his original master sent a message to his home saying, "A child of your house has returned from his travels." The people of his household were extremely happy, and planned to come and see him the following day. The master heard of this and said, "There is no end to the worldly dusts of the net of love. I have rejected this, and have left home. I do not wish to see them a second time." That night he packed his things and left.

After that, carrying his own water jug and staff, he travelled to every corner of the nation. He would always say, "Even if it is a

---

[7] Shui-hsiang yuan (Zuizo-in) literally means "the temple of the standing image". A *shui-hsiang* or standing image was a certain type of Buddha statue.

[8] Another term for the Buddha, literally meaning "thus come".

[9] This was after the death of Nan-ch'uan when Joshu was fifty-seven. The chronology followed in the biography is not very rigorous.

boy of seven years, if he is better than me, I will ask for his teaching. Even if it is a man of a hundred years, if he is not as good as me, I will instruct him."

When he reached the age of eighty he took up residence at Kuanyin yuan in the eastern part of Chao province.[10] The temple was about ten miles past the stone bridge. As the resident priest, the master emulated the ancients even though he became worn out and haggard in his old age. The monks' hall had no planks on the front or back. The mid-day meal was barely provided for. When one of the legs on his chair broke, he simply tied a piece of burned firewood to it. Once there was someone who wished to make a new leg for the chair, but the master would not permit it. The master was resident priest for forty years and never once was a letter sent out asking for support from the laity.

There was a monk from the south who had asked Hsueh-feng (Seppo),[11] "What about it when the waters of the ancient river valley are cold?"

Hsueh-feng said, "Though the eyes are wide open, the bottom is not seen."

The monk said, "What about the one who drinks of the water?"

Hsueh-feng said, "He does not take it in through his mouth."

The master heard of this and said, "He does not take it in through his mouth, he takes it in through his nose."

The monk then asked, "What about it when the waters of the ancient river valley are cold?"

The master said, "Bitter!"

The monk said, "What about the one who drinks of the water?"

The master said, "[He's] dead!"

Hsueh-feng heard of the master's words and said, "An old Buddha, an old Buddha", and offered nothing in response.

[10]   Chao-chou (Joshu) was a district in the present Hopeh. It is from the area in which his temple was located that Chao-chou receives the name he is known by.
[11]   Hsueh-feng I-tsun (Seppo Gizon, 822–908) was a disciple of Te-shan Hsuan-chien (Tokusan Senkan). He was one of the great masters of the late T'ang who lived in southern China and taught Ch'an (Zen) to large numbers of monks. His temple was in modern Fukien.

Some time later the King of Yen (En) of Hupei[12] led his troops in an attempt to invade the province of Chao. When the King of Yen had advanced to the borders of the province of Chao, an old man who happened to be there said, "In the state of Chao there is the dwelling of a holy man. If you make war against them, you will certainly be defeated."

Subsequently the King of Yen and the King of Chao held peace negotiations and agreed to maintain peace. The King of Yen asked, "In the fair land of Chao, who is the most wise?"

Someone said, "There is a priest who expounds the *Avatamsaka Sutra*. He is chaste and virtuous. If there is a year of great drought he goes to live on Mount T'ien-tai (Tendai) to pray by orders of the king, and before he returns sweet mercy has poured forth [from the sky]."

The King of Yen said, "Perhaps his goodness will be exhausted [if I call on him]."

Another person said, "About a hundred and twenty miles from here is Kuan-yin yuan. There there is a Ch'an (Zen) master who has led a virtuous life for many years and whose Wisdom Eye shines bright."

Everyone said, "This one certainly answers the description [of the most wise]."

The two kings directed their carts to go and see the master. When they arrived at the temple the master was sitting in meditation and did not get up from his seat [to greet them].

The King of Yen asked, "Are you to be honoured as a king of men, or as a king of the Dharma [the Truth of life]?"

The master said, "If I am a king of men, I am most honoured among the kings of men. If I am a king of the Dharma, I am most honoured among the kings of the Dharma."

The king nodded his approval.

The master sat quietly for a while then said, "Which of you is the King of Chao?"

---

[12] Yen (En) was the neighbouring province to Chao province.

The King of Chao identified himself.

The master said, "I am sorry but I have been completely immersed in the mountains and streams and have not managed to come and pay my respects to you."

The attendants of the two kings asked the master to expound the Dharma for the sake of the kings. The master said, "The attendants of the kings are many, yet how can they make me expound the Dharma?"

The kings then ordered their attendants to withdraw from the hall.

By the master's side at that time was a young novice named Wen-yuan[13] (Bun'en) who said in a loud voice, "I will inform the kings: you are not attendants."[14]

One of the kings asked, "What is an 'attendant'?"

Wen-yuan said, "The honourable names of the kings are many. The master does not venture to expound the Dharma for that reason."

The king said, "I request the master to disregard names and expound the Dharma."

The master said, "It is well known that the kings of the past ages of both your houses were enemies of the people. If I speak the name of the World-Honoured Buddha one time, the sins are expiated and blessings spring forth. It is because the forefathers of you kings were men who abused that name that the dissension [between you] was born."

The master's compassion was unflagging and he expounded the Dharma to them for many hours. When he was finished the kings bowed to the ground and gave thanks. At parting their gratitude was unbounded.

---

[13] Wen-yuan (Bun'en) was a disciple of Chao-chou who appears many times in the course of the text but about whom nothing else is known.

[14] The meaning here is that the king's family name includes those of his ancestors as becomes his position. These names are like "attendants" in that they have nothing to do with the real person.

By the next day the kings had returned to their own lands. When one of the captains of the king of Yen heard that the master did not rise [when the king had come], he rode all the way to the province of Chao early the next morning. Entering the temple, he ranted up and down, charging that the master had been condescending to his lord. The master heard of this and came out to talk with him.

The captain asked, "Yesterday you saw two kings come here, but you did not rise to greet them. Now you have seen me come, why is it that you come to greet me?"

The master said, "If you had managed to come like a king, I would not have got up to greet you either." When the captain heard the master's words he bowed three times and left.

Soon after that the King of Chao sent a message inviting the master to a banquet. When the master had arrived at the gate of the city, all the people [who lived there] met him and respectfully guided him on a tour of the interior. The master had barely dismounted from the carriage [that had been provided for him] when the king came and bowed, took the master into the palace, and requested he sit in his own [royal] seat at the head of the hall.

The master sat quietly for a while then, shading his eyes with his hand, he looked around the room and said, "You who stand here at the foot of the throne, what superintendent do you have?"

An attendant of the king answered, "The priests of all the temples, as well as great masters and wise men everywhere."

The master said, "Each of them is the master of one way of teaching. If they were at the foot of the throne, I too would rise to my feet and stand."

Thereupon the king sent orders for them [the priests] to come to the palace.

That day, towards the end of the feast, priests and officials were arranged in order from the head seat to the bottom seat, and each one asked one question in turn. One man asked about the Buddha-Dharma. The master looked at him and said, "What are you doing?"

The man said, "Asking about the Buddha-Dharma."

The master said, "Here, I am sitting down. There, you are asking, 'What is the Dharma?' Two masters do not teach side-by-side."[15]

The king then ended the questioning.

At that time the king and queen were standing to the left and right of the master. The queen asked, "I ask that the master place his hand on the head of the king and give him a blessing."

The master placed his hand on the head of the king and said, "I pray that the king lives to be of an age that equals my own."

At that time the master was escorted to an old temple nearby the palace and told to select ground for the construction of a new temple. When the master heard this he ordered a man to tell the king that "If one blade of grass is disturbed, I will leave the state of Chao."[16] At that time a soldier by the name of T'ou pledged to donate a tree garden worth 15,000 strings of cash. The name Chen-chi Ch'an-yuan (Shinzai Zen-in) was given to the temple. It was also known as the "T'ou family garden". After the master took up residence there, monks accumulated in large numbers.

Another time the King of Chao received a purple robe from the King of Yen to present to the master. When the king came to the district where the temple was, all the people went to meet him in the most reverential way, but the master firmly refused to go.

The king sent a messenger bearing a box who came before the master and said, "For the sake of the Buddha-Dharma, the king humbly requests the master to wear this robe."

The master said, "For the sake of the Buddha-Dharma, I will not wear this robe."

The messenger said, "To save the face of the king, you should wear it."

---

[15] The last sentence of Chao-chou's statement is from a text named the *Chin-tu lun* (*Chido-ron*). The meaning is that "besides sitting here, I have no other Dharma. I do not have two Dharmas at the same time."

[16] "If you build a new temple, I will leave; the old temple is sufficient for me." Thus, Chao-chou means, "If you disturb one more blade of grass than has already been disturbed ..."

The master said, "Then what job would you give me in the bureaucracy?"

The king then came in person and put the robe on the master's shoulders, paid homage and bowed three times.

The master simply nodded his assent.

The master dwelt in the district of Chen (Chin) for two years. When he was about to die, he gathered his disciples around him and said, "After I depart from the world and have been cremated, do not take any of the remains. Monks of the Ch'an (Zen) sect are not the same as the people of the world. The body is an apparent phenomenon; from what are the remains born? It cannot be permitted."

The master ordered one of his attendants to take his whisk to the King of Chao with the words, "I have not finished using this in my lifetime."

On the tenth day of the eleventh lunar month, in the year 897, the master assumed the full lotus position and passed away. At that time, the monks, lay people and carts, numbering over ten thousand, filled the T'ou family garden. The sounds of lamentation shook the meadows and fields. When the King of Chao had finished his mourning, he delivered his eulogy, saying, "There is no difference in the colourful adornments hiding the golden coffin of Kushinagara.[17] According to tradition, a tall stupa has been built, and a monument erected. I have given these the name 'the Stupa of Chenchi Ch'an-shih Kuang-tsu (Shinzai Zenji Koso)'."

In the year 953, on the seventeenth day of the fourth lunar month, while a monk was asking Hui-ts'ung Ch'an-shih[18] of Tung-yuan (Ezu Zenji of To-in) about the teaching of the former master Chaochou (Joshu), Hui-ts'ung bowed and left. He then took up his brush and wrote the foregoing account.

---

[17] Kushinagara was the name of the town where Shakyamuni Buddha passed into nirvana. The meaning of this is that the adornments of the coffin are apparently various and distinct, yet from the point of view of nirvana they are not different. The king is likening the coffin of Chao-chou and Chao-chou himself to the coffin of the Buddha and the Buddha.

[18] Hui-ts'ung (Ezu) was a disciple of Joshu who lived in Joshu's old temple Tung-yuan. There is nothing more known about him.

PART ONE

Lectures, Questions & Answers

1

The master asked Nan-ch'uan (Nansen),[1] "What is the Way?"

Nan-ch'uan said, "Ordinary mind is the Way."

The master said, "Then may I direct myself towards it or not?"

Nan-ch'uan said, "To seek [it] is to deviate [from it]."

The master said, "If I do not seek, how can I know about the Way?"

Nan-chu'an said, "The Way does not belong to knowing or not knowing. To know is to have a concept; to not know is to be ignorant. If you truly realize the Way of no doubt, it is just like the sky: wide open vast emptiness. How can you say 'yes' or 'no' to it?"

At these words the master had sudden enlightenment. His mind became like the clear moon.

1 Nan-ch'uan was the master of Chao-chou (Joshu).

2

Nan-ch'uan (Nansen) came to speak to the monks. The master asked, "Bright or dark?"[1]

Nan-ch'uan returned to his room.

The master left the hall and said, "At one question of mine that old priest was forced into silence and could not answer."

The head monk said, "Don't say that he was silent. It is only that you didn't understand."

The master struck him [with a stick] and said, "Actually, this blow should have been given to that old fool Nan-ch'uan himself."

1   Bright means differentiation, dark means sameness. These were commonly used terms in the Ch'an (Zen) circles of the T'ang dynasty. Chao-chou (Joshu) is asking, "Is there sameness or differentiation? Which will you speak about?"

3

The master asked Nan-ch'uan (Nansen), "Where does a person who knows what there is to know[1] go to?"

Nan-ch'uan said, "They go to be a water buffalo at the house of a lay person at the foot of the mountain."

The master said, "I am grateful for your instruction."

Nan-ch'uan said, "At midnight last night, the moonlight came through the window."

1   To be enlightened to the reality of the universe and oneself – of the interdependence of all existence. This "one great fact of interpenetrating causation" was the only aspect of Buddhist doctrine that all the various sects agreed upon in Chao-chou's (Joshu's) time.

4

Once the master was in charge of keeping the fires at the monastery. One day, while everyone was out tending the garden, the master went inside the monk's hall and shouted, "Help, fire! Help, fire!"

Everyone rushed back to the monk's hall, but the master had closed and barred the door. No one knew what to do. Finally, Nan-ch'uan (Nansen) took the key from its hook and threw it into the room through the window.[1]

1   In temples doors are locked from the outside.

5

Once when the master was drawing water from the well, he saw Nan-ch'uan (Nansen) passing by. Then, hanging on to a pillar, he extended his legs down into the well and shouted, "Save me! Save me!"

Nan-ch'uan held up a ladder and cried out, "One, two, three, four, five."

The master immediately got up and gave his thanks to Nan-ch'uan saying, "Just now, thanks to you, I was saved."

6

At Nan-ch'uan's (Nansen's) temple one day, the monks of both the east and west halls were arguing about a cat. Nan-ch'uan came into the room, held up the cat, and said, "If you can say something, I won't kill it. If you can't say anything, I'll kill it."

No one in the assembly could understand Nan-ch'uan's mind, so he killed the cat.

The next evening, the master returned from somewhere and, while they were exchanging greetings, Nan-ch'uan told him what happened and said, "What would you have done to save the cat?"

The master took off one of his sandals, put it on his head, and left.

Nan-ch'uan said, "If you had been there, the cat would have been saved."

7

The master asked Nan-ch'uan (Nansen), "I'm not asking about differentiation, what about sameness?"

Nan-ch'uan placed both hands on the ground [in the pose of a dog]. The master kicked him over, went to the infirmary, and shouted, "What a pity! What a pity!"

Nan-ch'uan heard this and sent someone to find out what the

trouble was. The master said, "It's a pity that I didn't get to kick him over a second time."

8

When Nan-ch'uan (Nansen) was coming back to his room after taking a bath, he saw the monk in charge of the bath stoking the fires and asked, "What are you doing?"

The monk answered, "Stoking the fire."

Nan-ch'uan said, "Don't forget to call the water buffalo in to have a bath."

The monk assented.

The next evening the monk came into Nan-ch'uan's room. Nan-ch'uan said, "What are you doing?"

The monk said, "Asking the water buffalo to come to the bath."

Nan-ch'uan said, "Did you bring a lead rope or not?"

The monk could not respond.

When the master came to call on Nan-ch'uan, Nan-ch'uan told him what had happened.

The master said, "I would have had something to say."

Nan-ch'uan said, "Well, have you brought a rope with you?"

The master came forward, grabbed him by the nose, and began pulling him to the bath house.

Nan-ch'uan said, "Okay! Okay! Beast!"

9

The master asked Nan-ch'uan (Nansen), "Please say something that is apart from the four statements and beyond the hundred negations."[1]

Nan-ch'uan returned to his room.

The master said, "That old priest. Every day he chatters and chatters, yet at this one question of mine he cannot say one word in reply."

The attendant said, "It is better if you do not say that he did not speak."

The master slapped him.

1   The four statements are "is", "is not", "both is and is not", "neither is nor is not". The one hundred negations are philosophical negations of any affirmative statement.

10

One day Nan-ch'uan (Nansen) shut the door to his room, made a circle around the door with ashes, and said to a monk, "If you can say something, I'll open the door."

Though there were many monks there, no one could understand Nan-ch'uan's mind.

Finally, the master came and said, "Good Heavens!"[1]

1   Expresses a meaning like "What's the matter?"

11

The master asked Nan-ch'uan (Nansen), "Mind is not Buddha, Wisdom is not the Way. Then is there any mistake or not?"

Nan-ch'uan said, "Yes, there is."

The master said, "Please tell me where the mistake is."

Nan-ch'uan said, 'Mind is not Buddha, Wisdom is not the Way."

The master left the room.

12

The master addressed the assembly saying, "This fact is clear and obvious. Even a person of limitless power cannot go beyond it. When I went to Kuei-shan's (Isan's)[1] place a monk asked him, 'What is the mind that the Patriarch[2] brought from the west?'[3] Kuei-shan said, 'Bring me my chair.' If he would be a master of our sect, he must begin to teach men by means of the fact of his own nature."

A monk then asked, "What is the mind that the Patriarch brought from the west?"

The master said, "Oak tree in the front garden."

The monk said, "Don't instruct by means of objectivity."

The master said, "I don't instruct by means of objectivity."

The monk again asked, "What is the mind that the Patriarch brought from the west?"

The master said, "Oak tree in the front garden."

1   Kuei-shan Ling-yu (Isan Reiyu, 771–883 CE) was a disciple of Po-chang Huai-hai (Hyakojo Ekai). He was co-founder of the Kuei-yang (Igyo) sect of Ch'an (Zen). His temple was in modern Hunan.
2   Bodhidharma, the Indian Buddhist monk who came to Canton around 520 CE and is named as the founder of Ch'an Buddhism.
3   He is asking, "What is the meaning of life?" The "mind" that the Patriarch brought is the realization of that meaning.

13

On another occasion the master said, "Ninety years ago I saw Ma-tsu (Baso)[1] who had more than eighty accomplished people[2] under him. Every one of them was a good Ch'an (Zen) person. They were not like the people of today who add branches and vines on top of branches and vines, all the time going far astray from the Truth. Later generations are not as good as the one that precedes them.

"For example, Nan-ch'uan (Nansen) always said, 'You must act being in the midst of differentiation and sameness.' Now what do you understand by this? The yellow-mouthed babies[3] of today talk of vines and creepers[4] on the main streets and highways, earning their living and looking for acclaim. Gathering assemblies of three hundred or five hundred monks they say, 'I am the accomplished person, you are the seeker'."

1   Ma-tsu Tao-i (Baso Doitsu, 709–788 CE) was a disciple of Nan-yueh Huai-jang (Nangaku Ejo) in the third generation from the Sixth Patriarch Hui-neng (Eno). Chao-chou's (Joshu's) own master, Nan-ch'uan, was a descendant of Ma-tsu.

2   *Akalvanamitra*, a Sanskrit word meaning your "closest friend", referring to a person who can inform you of, and liberate you from, your attachments and fetters and help you to the Buddha's Way.

3   A term of abuse.

4   "Vines and creepers" are explanations about the Ch'an (Zen) reality.

14

A monk asked, "What is the pure undefiled *sangha*?"[1]
  The master said, "A girl in pig-tails."[2]
  The monk asked, "What are the people in the sangha?"
  The master said, "The girl in pig-tails is pregnant."

1   The *sangha* is the community of monks and nuns, and more specifically the place where they live.

2   In China boys and girls who were virgins wore their hair in pig-tails.

15

A monk asked, "I've heard that you met intimately with Nan-ch'uan (Nansen), is it not so?"
  The master said, "In the province of Chen[1] large radishes are produced."

1   A neighbouring district that was famous for its radishes.

16

A monk asked, "Where were you born?"
  The master pointed with his hand, faced towards the west, and said, "West".

17

A monk asked, "'The Dharma is not a special Dharma'. What is the Dharma?"[1]
  The master said, "Nothing outside; nothing inside. Nothing inside and outside."

1 The source of the quotation is unknown. This is a stock question that monks asked at the time.

18

A monk asked, "What is the true *Dharmakaya*[1] of the Buddha?"
The master said, "Is there anything else you don't like?"

1 Indian Buddhist philosophy developed the idea of a *Buddhakaya*, Buddha nature or "body", which has three aspects. The *Dharmakaya*, lit. "truth-body", is one of these three aspects and is the *Dharma* or truth that is the universal aspect and pure essence of the *Buddhakaya*.

19

A monk asked, "What is the Dharma gate of the mind?"[1]
The master said, "The examples of the past and present."[2]

1 The question means, "What is the entrance into experiencing the reality of the universe (mind)?"
2 The word "example" was conventionally used to refer to men who passed the examinations and received positions in the government. They were "examples" to others to study hard to pass exams themselves. Chao-chou (Joshu) is using the word to refer to the Ch'an (Zen) masters of the past and present, and is presenting himself as the example here and now of the Dharma gate of the mind.

20

A monk asked, "What is the host amidst the guest?"[1]
The master said, "I do not ask for a wife."
The monk said, "What is the guest amidst the host?"
The master said, "I have no father-in-law."

1 One of the four positions of host and guest: host as host, guest as guest, host amidst guest, guest amidst host. These were made famous by Lin-chi (Rinzai). They illustrate the reality of subject and object.

A monk asked, "What is it in which all the dharmas[1] eternally abide?"

The master said, "I don't give names to the Patriarchs."

The monk repeated his question.

The master said, "Today, I'll give no answer."

1 Every phenomenon in the universe has its own unique nature, its own truth. This quality of each thing is called its *dharma*, and is relative to the truth of the totality of life called the *Dharma*.

22

The master entered the hall to address the assembly and said, "Brothers, don't stand around so long. If you have some problem, let's discuss it. If you have no problem, then go sit and delve into the Truth. When I was on my own pilgrimages, I went without the two meals;[1] they are a place of confusion for the mind's energy to go. If you are not like that, you are a long way from being a monk who has 'left home'."

1 The Buddhist custom is to eat twice a day: in the morning and at midday. In modern times, a medicinal meal was added in the evening.

23

A monk asked, "Among the ten thousand things, which is the most solid?"

The master said, "When we curse at each other, that we can go on flapping our lips. When we spit at each other, that we can have our saliva flow out."

24

A monk asked, "What about it when morning to evening is a continuous flow?"

The master said, "For a monk there is nothing like the two taxations[1] on the populace."

1 In China, taxes were collected twice a year and were very hard on the people. The times of hardship are used to differentiate the passage of time.

25

A monk asked, "What is the one word?"[1]

The master said, "If you hold on to one word it will make an old man of you."

1 The one word which sums up the reality of the universe, the fact of your own experience.

26

The master entered the hall to address the assembly and said, "Brothers, if for your entire life you do not leave the monastery, and if you do not speak for five or ten years, there is no one who would call you someone who cannot speak. Beyond this, what could even a Buddha do to you? If you do not believe [what I say], you can cut off my head."

27

The master entered the hall and said, "Brothers, you are certainly in the third world of karmic retribution.[1] For this reason there is the saying, 'Only remake the deeds of the past, don't remake the person of the past'.[2] Each of us has left our own homes, and has become carefree.

"Furthermore, we ask about Zen and ask about the Way. Twenty or thirty of us come together and ask. However, it looks very likely that you are lacking Zen and the Way. Though you call me an 'accomplished person', I have received the same sentence as you.[3]

I'm not a good talker and don't want to get bogged down with the ancients, so I talk about the east and talk about the west."

1 This refers to the birth as a human being in this world, but why it is called this is unclear.
2 The source of the reference is unknown.
3 The sentence of being born in the 'third world of karmic retribution'.

28

A monk asked, "During the twenty-four hours, how is mind put to use?"

The master said, "You are used by the twenty-four hours; I use the twenty-four hours. Which of these 'times' are you talking about?"

29

A monk asked, "What is Chao-chou's (Joshu's) master?"[1]
The master shouted, "You hooped barrel!"
The monk answered, "Yes?"[2]
The master said, "A well-done hooped barrel."

1 Literally the word means "hero" or "master". Here the word means "true self" or "real person".
2 The monk answers as if his name has been called.

30

A monk asked, "What is the fact of my nature?"[1]
The master said, "Shake the tree and the birds take to the air, startle the fish and the water becomes muddy."

1 See also no. 12.

31

A monk asked, "What is an imbecile?"[1]

The master said, "I'm not as good as you."

The monk said, "I'm not trying to be anything."

The master said, "Why are you an imbecile?"

1   This comes from the statement by Nan-ch'uan (Nansen): "For a moment do not submit to sight, hearing, or thinking. Naturally you are like a moron or an imbecile. To be without knowledge of the hundreds of goings-on is best."

32

A monk asked, "'The True Way is without difficulty, just refrain from picking and choosing.'[1] The men of today make 'nests and burrows' don't they?"[2]

The master said, "Once I was asked about this, but it's been five years now and I still can't define it."

1   This is a quotation from the *Treatise on Being True to Mind* (*Hsin-hsin ming*).
2   "Nests and burrows", "picking and choosing" and "defining" all refer to making distinctions.

33

There was an official who asked, "Tan-hsia (Tanka) burned a wooden Buddha image. Why did the head priest's eyebrows fall out?"[1]

The master said, "In your house, who is it that transforms raw vegetables into cooked vegetables?"

The official said, "The servant."

The master said, "Well, he is quite skilful."

1   Tan-hsia T'ien-jan (Tanka Tennen) was a disciple of Shih-t'ou (Sekito). There is a famous story about him going into a temple one bitterly cold winter's day, taking a Buddha statue off its dais and setting it on fire to warm himself (and the other monks). When the abbot of the temple heard of this, he came running and tried to put out the fire, asking Tan-hsia what he was doing.

Tan-hsia said, "I'm trying to obtain the holy remains of the Buddha."

The abbot said, "How can you obtain the holy remains from a wooden-Buddha statue?"

Tan-hsia said, "If there are no holy remains, let's burn the other statues also."

Because of this conversation the abbot's eyebrows fell out, which happens when you falsely expound the doctrine.

34

A monk asked, "What about it when the hermit T'i-mu (Bimoku) took hold of Shan-tsai's (Zenzai's) hand and an ethereal Buddha appeared to him?"[1]

The master took hold of the monk's hand and said, "What do you see?"

1 In the *Avatamsaka Sutra*, Manjushri, the Buddhist *bodhisattva*, or demi-god, of wisdom instructs Shan-tsai to travel to the south. There he visits fifty-three holy men, the ninth of whom is T'i-mu.

35

There was a nun who asked, "What is the practice of a sangha member?"

The master said, "Don't bear any children."

The nun said, "If not for you, there would be no involvements."

The master said, "If I had some involvement with you, what could you do to withstand it?"

36

A monk asked, "What is Chao-chou's (Joshu's) master?"[1]

The master said, "You stupid oaf!"

1 See also no. 29.

37

A monk asked, "What is the king's search for a *saidhava*?"[1]

The master said, "Did you say you needed me here for something?"

1 In the *Nirvana Sutra*, the king searches for a *saidhava*, a wise servant who could understand the king's mind clearly.

38

A monk asked, "What is the depth of the deep?"

The master said, "What depth of the deep should I talk about, the seven of seven or the eight of eight?"

39

A monk asked, "What is a saidhava?"[1]

The master said, "A quiet place – *Svaha!*"[2]

1 See no. 37.
2 *Svaha* is a Sanskrit word (Japanese *sowaka*) that comes at the end of many mantras and sutras. It means roughly "so be it" and is like "Amen".

40

A monk asked, "What is a dharma that is not a dharma?"[1]

The master said, "South, north, east, west."

The monk said, "How is this to be understood?"

The master said, "Up, down, and the four directions."[2]

1 In the *Vajracchedika Sutra*, there is a passage, "All the dharmas are not any dharma at all. Therefore, they are called 'all the dharmas'."
2 South-east, south-west, north-east, north-west.

41

A monk asked, "What is the depth of the deep?"[1]

The Master said, "If you are there, you are certanly seventy-four or seventy-five years old."[2]

1 See also no. 38.
2 Probably the age of the monk who asked the question.

42

A monk asked, "What was the king's search for *saidhava*?"

The master suddenly stood up with his hands folded on his chest.[1]

1 The traditional posture for monks when standing in attendance.

43

A monk asked, "What is the Way?"

The master said, "You're too kind!"[1]

1 The phrase used is the customary response to "thank you". Chao-chou (Joshu) is using it here as an example of an ordinary word.

44

A monk asked, "What is the Dharma?"

The master said, "*Ch'ih-ch'ih she-she.*"[1]

1 A phrase used in China at the Taoist New Year ceremonies to drive out evil spirits and portents.

45

A monk asked, "How far is it from the province of Chao to the province of Chen?"

The master said, "Three hundred miles."

The monk asked, "How far is it from the province of Chen to

the province of Chao?"

The master said, "No distance."

46

A monk asked, "What is the depth of the deep?"

The master said, "How long has there been a 'deep'?"

The monk said, "The deep has been here for ever."

The master said, "Fortunately, you met me; you almost became someone who was 'deeped' to death."

47

A monk asked, "What is my self?"

The master said, "Well, do you see the oak tree in the front garden?"[1]

1   See no. 12.

48

The master entered the hall and said, "If you are someone who has long practised you are not without the reality, and you see into the past and present. If you are someone who has newly entered the assembly, you must begin to investigate the Truth.

"Don't just chase around [living off] the assemblies of three hundred, five hundred or a thousand monks, and the rest of the sangha. If you praise someone saying, 'Oh, he's a good priest', and even if you ask him about the Buddha-Dharma, still it is like frying gravel to eat as food. You are not able to do anything about what he says, you can't even open your own mouth [to reply].

"On the other hand, if you say, 'He is wrong, I am right', your face will turn bright red with shame and you will be making blasphemous statements in the world.

"If you sincerely strive to be clear about that mind [which neither praises nor blames], you will not have wronged me."

49

A monk asked, "To be in the secular world speaking about the Dharma on behalf of all the holy men is simply to be dependent on ornaments and artifices. It is not clear to me, how do you instruct people?"

The master said, "Where do you see me?"

The monk said, "Please tell me."

The master said, "None of the monks in this whole hall understands what you're saying."

A different monk asked, "Please tell me."

The master said, "You speak, I'll listen."

50

A monk asked, "It is said, 'The true teaching leaves no traces'. What about it when there is no teacher and no disciple?"

The master said, "Who made you come and ask this?"

The monk said, "Not someone else."

The master struck him.

51

A monk asked, "How is this fact[1] known about?"

The master said, "I think you're a little odd."

The monk said, "How do you know?"

The master said, "Whether it's accepting the responsibility[2] or not, you must see for yourself."

1 The fact of one's own nature, one's own reality.
2 Accepting the responsibility of one's own experience and living life.

52

A monk asked, "What is a man of no knowledge?"

The master said, "What are you talking about?"

53

A monk asked, "What is the mind that the Patriarch brought from the west?"

The master got up from his seat.

The monk said, "Is it nothing more than this?"

The master said, "I haven't said anything yet."

54

A monk asked, "The Buddha-Dharma is eternal, how is the mind put to use?"

The master said, "Take a look at the times of the Former Han and Later Han [dynasties], the empire was well governed; but when the emperor was about to die, not even half a copper coin was left undivided."

55

A monk asked, "Men of today are honoured because of their wealth. For what is a sangha member honoured?"

The master said, "Shut your mouth right now."

The monk said, "If I shut my mouth, do I have it or not?"

The master said, "If you don't shut your mouth, how will you realize it?"

56

A monk asked, "What is Chao-chou's (Joshu's) one word?"[1]

The master said, "There is not even half a word."

The monk said, "Can it be that you have none?"[2]

The master said, "I am not one word."

1   See also no. 25.
2   "Could it be that you can't say it?"

57

A monk asked, "How can you not lead the multitudes of the world astray?"

The master stuck out his foot.

The monk took off one of the master's sandals.

The master brought back his foot.

The monk could say nothing more.

58

There was an official who asked, "In the days of the Buddha, all living things took shelter in the Buddha. After the Buddha entered nirvana, in what did all living things take shelter?"

The master said, "There are no living things."

The official said, "Even as I ask [this]?"

This master said, "What other Buddha do you seek?"

59

A monk asked, "Is there anyone who is requiting the four kindnesses[1] in the three worlds?"[2]

The master said, "There is."

The monk said, "What sort of person is he?"

The master said, "You parent killer! This one question shows you are lacking."

1   The kindness of the Three Treasures (Buddha, Dharma, Sangha), the kindness of the emperor, the kindness of parents, the kindness of all living things.
2   The world of desire, the world of form, the world of no form.

60

A monk asked, "What is your intention?"

The master said, "There is no method to it."

61

The master entered the hall and said, "Brothers, simply remake what has gone by and work with what comes. If you do not remake, you are stuck deeply somewhere."

62

Another time the master said, "I have been here more than thirty years. Not yet has one Ch'an (Zen) man ever come here. Even if one did come, after staying a night and grabbing a meal, he would quickly move on, heading for a warm and comfortable place."

A monk asked, "If a Ch'an man happened to come here, what would you say to him?"

The master said, "The thousand-pound stone bow[1] is not used to shoot a mouse."

1 A large war bow that shot heavy stones and took a man of enormous strength to shoot it.

63

Another time the master said, "Brothers, if someone comes from the south, then I unburden him. If someone comes from the north, I load him up. Therefore, it is said, 'If you go to a superior man to ask about the Way, the Way is lost. If you go to an inferior man to ask about the Way, the Way is gained.'"

64

Another time, the master said, "Brothers, if a truthful man

expounds a heresy, that heresy is the truth. If a heretical man expounds the True Dharma, the True Dharma becomes a heresy.

"Everywhere it[1] is hard to see but easy to know about. Where I am it is easy to see but hard to know about."

1   Ch'an (Zen).

65

A monk asked, "Has someone who cannot be taken in by 'good and bad' liberated himself or not?"

The master said, "He has not liberated himself."

The monk said, "Why has he not liberated himself?"

The master said, "Obviously he exists in good and bad."

66

A nun asked, "Setting aside the explanations given until now, please instruct me."

The master shouted, "Burn an iron bottle to ashes!"

The nun then went and poured the water out of an iron bottle and brought it to the master saying, "Please answer."

The master laughed at this.

67

A monk asked, "It is said that the world will change into a black hole. It is not clear to me, what course will this[1] follow?"

The master said, "It is not foretold."

The monk said, "Who is it that does not foretell?"

The master said, "[You] stupid oaf!"

1   The basic reality of the universe.

68

A monk asked, "It is said, 'Without words and without thinking, you can begin to make a statement.'[1] Without words, what do you call a statement?"

The master said, "High yet not dangerous, full yet not overflowing."[2]

The monk said, "Right now, are you full or overflowing?"

The master said, "How is it that you ask me that?"

1 The source of this reference is not known.
2 Chao-chou (Joshu) is quoting from the *Book of Filial Piety*.

69

A monk asked, "What is that which is spiritual?"

The master said, "A puddle of piss in the Pure Land."

The monk said, "I ask you to reveal it to me."

The master said, "Don't tempt me."

70

A monk asked, "'The Dharmakaya[1] does nothing, it does not fall into the various categories.'[2] Then can you talk about it or not?"

The master said, "How have you been able to talk about it?"

The monk said, "In that case, I have not spoken."

The master laughed at this.

1 See no. 18.
2 From the *Vimalikirti-nirdesa Sutra*.

71

The monk asked, "What is Buddha, and what is all living things?

The master said, "All living things are Buddha, Buddha is all living things."

The monk asked, "It is not yet clear to me, of those two which is 'all living things'?"

The master said, "Ask me."

72

A monk asked, "'The Great Way has no root';[1] how can it be expressed?"

The master said, "You just expressed it."

The monk said, "What about 'no root'?"

The master said, "There is no root. Where is it that you are being bound up?"

1 The source of the reference is unknown.

73

A monk asked, "I wonder if a man of true practice can be perceived by gods and demons or not?"

The master said, "They can perceive him."

The monk said, "Where is his fault?"

The master said, "Faults are wherever they are looked for."

The monk said, "In that case, it is not practice."

The master said, "It is practice."

74

A monk asked, "The solitary moon is in the sky, from where does its light emanate?"

The master said, "From where does the moon emanate?"

75

A monk asked, "I've heard that you have said, 'The Way is not acquired by practice, just don't become degenerate.' What is not being degenerate?"

The master said, "Closely examining inside and outside."

The monk said, "Then do you yourself closely examine or not?"

The master said, "I closely examine."

The monk said, "What fault do you have that you yourself closely examine?"

The master said, "What is it[1] that you have?"

1 "What is the 'fact' that you also have?"

76

The master entered the hall and said, "This fact is like a clear jewel in your hand. If a barbarian comes, it reveals a barbarian. If a Chinese comes, it reveals a Chinese."

77

Another time the master said, "I can make one blade of grass be a sixteen-foot golden Buddha,[1] and I can make a sixteen-foot gold Buddha be one blade of grass. Buddha is compulsive passions,[2] compulsive passions are Buddha."

A monk asked, "For the sake of whom does Buddha become compulsive passions?"

The master said, "For the sake of all people Buddha becomes compulsive passions."

The monk said, "How can they be escaped?"

The master said, "What's the use of escaping?"

1 A particular type of Buddha statue was sixteen feet tall.
2 The first two of the Four Noble Truths of Buddhism are (1) life is suffering, (2) suffering is caused by compulsive passions.

78

The master instructed the assembly saying, "Right here I am teaching people by means of my own nature. If I had to teach people according to their own root nature, I would naturally use the doctrines for the three types and twelve divisions[1] to teach them. If you do not understand them [the doctrines], whose fault is it?

"After this, whenever I meet a good Ch'an (Zen) person, I will say, 'I have not wronged him'. Whoever it is who questions me, I will teach him by means of my own nature."

1   The three types are: hearer, *arhat* (one who has saved him/herself), and *bodhisattva* (one who has delayed nirvana to help others to enlightenment). The twelve divisions are the various teachings given by the Buddha adapted to suit people of different natures and capacities.

79

A monk asked, "From long ago until now, it has been said that 'mind is Buddha'.[1] Will you allow me to discuss 'not mind' or not?"

The master said, "Setting aside mind, what is there to discuss?"

1   A famous statement by Ma-tsu Tao-i (Baso Doitsu).

80

A monk asked, "The ancient mirror[1] is not polished, then does it shine or not?"

The master said, "The previous life is the cause, the present life is the effect."

1   The original nature, the true self.

81

A monk asked, "What about it when the three-pronged sword[1] has not yet fallen?"

The master said, "Densely packed together."

The monk said, "What about after it has fallen?"

The master said, "Wide open spaces."

1   The three-pronged sword could be a metaphor for the three worlds or three times, but it is not clear from the context. The meaning of the question is "Before the world of time and space has been discriminated (created), what about it?"

82

A monk asked, "What is a man who gets out of the three worlds?"
The master said, "He can't be trapped."

83

A monk asked, "When Nui-t'ou (Gozu) had not yet met the Fourth Patriarch,[1] all the birds held flowers in their mouths and gave offerings to each other. After he met him, why did all the birds not hold flowers in their mouths and make offerings to each other?"

The master said, "At one with the world, not at one with the world."

1   Nui-t'ou Fa-jung (Gozu Hoyu, 594–657 CE) received the transmission of the Dharma from the Fourth Patriarch Tao-hsin (Doshin, 580–651) but is not considered to be in the orthodox line of succession even though he set up his own line of teaching. The long story of their meeting is in the *Records of the Transmission of the Lamp*. The question is asking about the nature of the enlightenment experience.

84

A monk asked, "What about it when a white cloud is independent?"
The master said, "How can you be at ease everywhere like a calm spring wind?"

85

A monk asked, "What is the white ox in the open ground?"[1]
The master said, "The moonlight uses no colours."

The monk said, "What things does it [the ox] eat?"

The master said, "Past and present, it has eaten nothing."

The monk said, "Please say something about it."

The master said, "I am obviously doing so."

1   The reference is to the *Saddharma Pundarika Sutra*. A rich man, whose children are heedlessly playing in their burning house, tries to lure the children out of the house by various means. The white ox cart is finally the means whereby all are lured out of the house to safety. The "white ox in the open ground" then symbolizes the teaching that can free people from the world of suffering caused by compulsive passions and lead them to enlightenment. The monk is not, however, asking for such an analogy.

86

The master addressed the assembly saying, "To seek for mind is to deviate from it."[1]

A monk asked, "What about it when mind is not sought?"

The master struck him three times and said, "I have not wronged you."

1   See no. 1.

87

A monk asked, "Usually when there are questions and answers, the intellect is involved. Without being involved with intellect, how will you respond?"

The master said, "Ask a question."

The monk said, "Please say something."

The master said, "Don't bring good and bad here."

88

A monk asked, "The Dragon King's daughter paid her personal homage to the Buddha.[1] It's not clear to me, how did she pay homage?"

The master pressed his hands together in the attitude of paying homage.

1   In the *Saddharma Pundarika Sutra* the Dragon King's eight-year-old daughter took a jewel worth three thousand worlds as homage to give to the Buddha. Immediately upon giving it she became Buddha herself.

89

The master instructed the assembly saying, "As for the Buddha-Dharma of this place: if you say it's easy, it's difficult. If you say it's difficult, it's easy. Somewhere else, it is difficult to see yet easy to know about. Where I am, it is easy to see yet difficult to know about. If you can understand this, you can go against the grain of the world.

"If a man asks you, 'Where have you come from?', and you say to him, 'I've come from Chao-chou (Joshu)', then you have slandered Chao-chou. If you say to him, 'I have not come from Chao-chou', you are slighting yourself. All of you, just how will you answer?"

A monk asked, "To sock you in the eye is to slander you. How is it possible to act without slandering you?"

The master said, "If you say it is not a slander, it is immediately a slander."

90

A monk asked, "What is the path of true practice?"

The master said, "If you know how to practise, do it. If you do not know how to practise, you'll probably fall into some world of cause and effect."

The master instructed the assembly saying, "I will teach you how to speak. If there is time when someone questions you, just say, 'I've come from Chao-chou (Joshu).' If he asks, 'What does Chao-chou say about the Dharma?', just say to him, 'When it's cold, he says it's cold; when it's hot, he says it's hot'. If he further asks, 'I wasn't asking about that kind of thing', just say to him 'What kind of thing were you asking about?' If again he says, 'What does Chao-chou say about the Dharma?', just say, 'When I left the master, he did not give me any message to pass on to you. If you must know about Chao-chou's affairs, go ask him yourself.'"

92

A monk asked, "What about it when I look neither in front nor behind?"

The master said, "Setting aside looking neither in front nor behind, who are you questioning?"

93

The master instructed the assembly saying, "Kashyapa[1] transmitted it to Ananda.[2] Tell me, whom did Bodhidharma transmit it to?"

A monk asked, "Supposing that the Second Patriarch 'got the marrow',[3] what about it?"

The master said, "Don't slander the Second Patriarch."

The master then said, "Bodhidharma had a saying, 'Someone who is outside attains the skin; someone who is inside attains the bone.' Tell me, what has the one who is inside attained?"

A monk asked, "What is the truth of 'attaining the marrow'?"

The master said, "Simply be aware of the skin, where I am the marrow is not established."

The monk said, "What is the marrow?"

The master said, "In that case, the skin too is sought and not found."

1 Kashyapa was the Second Patriarch of Ch'an (Zen) in India.

2 Ananda was the successor of Kashyapa and the Third Patriarch of Ch'an in India.

3 The "Second Patriarch" always refers to Hui-k'o (Eka) who was the Second Patriarch of Ch'an in China. Bodhidharma, the Twenty-eighth Patriarch of Ch'an in India and the First Patriarch of it in China, said that he had four types of disciples: those who realized the skin, those who realized the muscle, those who realized the bone, and those who realized the marrow of his teaching. Hui-k'o was the only one who got the marrow.

94

A monk asked, "Just as it is, so clear and present. How can it not be your 'universal position'?"[1]

The master said, "Do you know that there is someone who does not permit it to be so?"

The monk said, "In that case, he is at a different position."

The master said, "Who is he who is at a different position?"

The monk said, "Who is he who is not different?"

The master said, "Call him whatever you like."

1 The "universal position" is one of the "five positions" devised by Tung-shan (Tozan). It is the position of universality as opposed to particularity.

95

A monk asked, "To a superior man, make one action and he moves on. What about when an inferior man comes?"

The master said, "Are you superior or inferior?"

The monk said, "Please answer."

The master said, "In speaking you are not yet the master."

The monk said, "I've come seven thousand miles, don't play mind games with me."

The master said, "I have received this question from you so how can mind games not be played?"

The monk stayed one night and left.

96

A monk said, "What about someone who does not follow anything that is peripheral?"[1]

The master said, "Who are you?"

The monk said, "Hui-yen (E'en)."

The master said, "What did you ask?"

The monk said, "About someone who does not follow anything that is peripheral."

The master patted him on the head.

1   Irrelevant or non-essential to Ch'an (Zen).

97

A monk asked, "What is the fact of the 'handing on of the robe'?"[1]

The master said, "Don't deceive yourself."

1   The transmission of the Dharma.

98

A monk asked, "'True Reality', 'ordinary', and 'holy' are all dream words. What is a true word?"

The master said, "Don't say anything more about these two."

The monk said, "Setting aside these two, what is a true word?"

The master said, "*An-pu-lin-fa.*"[1]

1   A mantra from a tantric scripture (Japanese *An-bu-rin-patsu*). A mantra of this sort has no meaning other than the sound. The tantric sect of Buddhism in China was called the True Word sect.

99

A monk asked, "What is Chao-chou (Joshu)?"

The master said, "East gate, west gate, south gate, north gate."

100

A monk asked, "What is meditation?"[1]

The master said, "It is not meditation."

The monk said, "Why is it 'not meditation'?"

The master said, "It's alive, it's alive!"

1   The Japanese word *zen* comes from Chinese *ch'an* which comes from the
     Indian Sanskrit *dhyana* which means "meditation". The character translated
     here refers more specifically to the act of doing meditation as a special prac-
     tice in contrast to the other activities of daily life. Dhyana refers to meditation
     as a state of mind that is present in all the affairs of daily living.

101

A monk asked, "What about it when I'm not chasing after various
things?"

The master said, "Obviously, it is just like this."

The monk said, "Isn't this the fact of my own nature?"

The master said, "Chasing, chasing."

102

A monk asked, "In thirty years an ancient wise man only managed
to shoot half a man with one bow and two arrows.[1] Today I ask
the master to shoot perfectly."

The master immediately stood up.

1   The reference is to a story about Shih-kung Hui-ts'ang (Sekkyo Ezo) – a
     descendant of Ma-tsu (Baso) – and a monk named San-p'ing (San pei). San-
     p'ing came to see Shih-kung but, before he had come through the door, Shih-
     kung made the motion of drawing a bow and said, "Look, the arrow!"

San-p'ing thrust out his chest and said, "Is it an arrow that kills or an arrow that gives life?"

Shih-kung then pulled the bow string three times and San pei bowed three times.

Shih-kung said, "I've spent thirty years with one bow and two arrows; today I've managed to shoot half a man." Shih-kung then broke his bow and arrows.

103

The master instructed the assembly saying, "'The True Way is without difficulty, just refrain from picking and choosing.'[1] To talk about it even a little is picking and choosing. Yet, I am not within 'pure clarity'.[2] In what place can you see the Patriarch?"[3]

A monk asked, "You are not within 'pure clarity', so what place are you attentive to?"

The master said, "I don't know either."

The monk said, "You yourself do not know, so how can you say you are not within 'pure clarity'?"

The master said, "Your question has been good. Now make your bow and retire."

1 See no. 32.
2 In the *Shinjin-mei* (*Hsin-hsin ming*; *Treatise on Being True to Mind*) "pure clarity" is the opposite of "picking and choosing". It is the state of mind of non-discrimination.
3 This could refer to the Third Patriarch, Seng-ts'an (Sosan), or it could refer to all the Patriarchs. The meaning is "how do you realize the mind of the Patriarch(s)?"

104

The master instructed the assembly saying, "'The Dharma originally is unborn, right now it is undying.'[1] Nothing more need be said. To speak a little bit is 'giving birth'. To not speak is 'dying'. All of you, just what will you do about this unborn and dying truth?"

A monk asked, "Right now[2] was it unborn and dying?"

The master said, "This fellow can see only dead words."

1   From the *Vimalikirti-nirdesa Sutra*.
2   Refers to what Chao-chou (Joshu) said.

105

A monk asked, "'The True Way is without difficulty, just refrain from picking and choosing.'[1] To talk about it even a little is 'picking and choosing'. How, then, do you instruct people?"

The master said, "Why do you not finish quoting the words of the ancient?"

The monk said, "I only can say until that point."

The master said, "Only that 'The True Way is without difficulty, just refrain from picking and choosing' [is my instruction]."

1   See no. 103.

106

The master entered the hall to instruct the assembly and said, "Reading sutras is still within birth and death. Not reading the sutras is also within birth and death. All of you, right now what will you do to get out of birth and death?"

A monk asked, "Supposing neither is done, what about it?"

The master said, "If true, it is all right. If that's not true, how can you get out of birth and death?"

107

A monk asked, "What about it when the blade of a sharp sword is keen?"

The master said, "I am a sharp sword. Where is the keenness?"

108

A monk asked, "When great difficulties come upon us how can they be avoided?"

The master said, "Well come!"[1]

1   "They've come at the right time", "Bring them on".

109

The master entered the hall and, after sitting quietly for a while, said, "Is everyone here or not?"

Someone said, "Everyone is here."

The master said, "I'm waiting for one more to come, then I'll speak."

A monk said, " I will tell you that you are waiting for a person who does not come."

The master said, "It's a person that's really hard to find."

110

The master instructed the assembly saying, "'If mind is born, the myriad dharmas are born. If the mind dies, the myriad dharmas die.'[1] All of you, what will you do about this?"

A monk asked, "Supposing there is neither birth nor death, what about it?"

The master said, "That's a good question."

1   From the *Treatise on Awakening of Faith* (*Ch'i-hsin lun*).

111

Once while speaking the master said, "'Bright is not bright, to say dark is to make it light.'[1] Which side are you on?"[2]

A monk said, "On neither side."

The master said, "In that case, you're in the middle."

The monk said, "If in the middle, I would be on both sides."

The master said, "How long have you been at my place? Though you talk like that, you have not managed to get beyond the three statements.[3] Even supposing that you are let outside of them, still you would be in the three statements. So what will you do?"

The monk said, "I can use the three statements."

The master said, "Why didn't you say so sooner?"

1   The source of the reference is not clear.
2   Bright or dark. Bright is differentiation, dark is sameness.
3   The three statements may be bright, dark and the interfusion of bright and dark. This formula was popular at the time in Ch'an (Zen) discussion.

112

A monk asked, "What is 'travelling through the world'?"
The master said, "Leaving 'diamond Ch'an'."[1]

1   "Diamond Ch'an" may refer to the attitude of staying in one place and having a concentrated practice rather than a practice that related to the business of the world of society, but it is not clear what Chao-chou (Joshu) is referring to as "diamond Ch'an".

113

The master instructed the assembly saying, "All of you monks, you must simply begin to cut off the heads of the Sambhogakaya and Nirmanakaya Buddhas."[1]

A monk asked, "What is a man who cuts off the heads of the Sambhogakaya and Nirmanakaya Buddhas?"

The master said, "Not in your world."

1   In Buddhist philosophy there are three bodies of the Buddha: the Dharmakaya, which is the universal aspect, i.e. pure essence, truth; the Nirmanakaya, which is the apparent forms aspect, i.e. the material world of changing forms; and the Sambhogakaya which is the responsive aspect, i.e. the emotional/psychological experiences that arise from the interplay between the Dharmakaya and the Nirmanakaya and which create the fabric of cause and effect.

114

The master instructed the assembly saying, "'The great way is right before your eyes. But actually it is hard to see.'"[1]

A monk asked, "What form has that which is before our eyes? Show it to me."

The master said, "Honan or Hopei, as you please."[2]

The monk said, "Then have you no means to help people?"

The master said, "What did you ask me about a moment ago?"

1　The reference is to the *Song of the Mahayana* (*T'a-ch'eng ts'an*) by Hoshi (Pao-chih).

2　Honan and Hopei were the two major provinces of China in those days. Chao-chou (Joshu) is saying "anywhere, wherever you wish, you can see it".

115

A monk asked, "When the Dharma realm is entered, is it known about or not?"

The master said, "Who enters into the Dharma realm?"

The monk said, "In that case, the entering into the Dharma realm is not known about."

The master said, "There are not even the cold ashes of a dead tree, clumps of flowers in hundreds of varieties just as they are."

The monk said, "Isn't this the expression of the state of having entered into the Dharma realm?"

The master said, "What relationship could there be?"[1]

1　"They're unrelated" is what Chao-chou (Joshu) is saying.

116

A monk asked, "If this is the True Realm of Reality, where did it come from?"

The master said, "Please say that one more time."

A monk asked, "The ten thousand things arise together,[1] then is there anyone who is not deluded [by them]?"

The master said, "There is."

The monk said, "What is he who is not deluded?"

The master said, "Do you believe that there is a Buddha-Dharma or not?"

The monk said, "I believe there is a Buddha-Dharma, the ancients have said so. What is he who is not deluded?"

The master said, "Why don't you ask me?"

The monk said, "I did ask."

The master said, "Deluded."

1   Are involved with each other, interdependent.

A monk asked, "It is not yet clear to me, men of the past and men of today, are we[1] close to each other or not?"

The master said, "To be close to each other is to be close to each other, but it is not to be of the same substance."

The monk said, "Why are we not the same?"

The master said, "The Dharmakaya does not talk of the Dharma."

The monk said, "The Dharmakaya does not talk of the Dharma, then do you help people or not?"

The master said, "I answer out of kindness."

The monk said, "Then why do you say, 'The Dharmakaya does not expound the Dharma'?"

The master said, "Through kindness I have sought for your papa,[2] but at last he did not stick his head out."

1   The monk is referring to himself.
2   The reference is to the "men of the past".

A monk asked, "I am speaking about the time when we haven't met each other; is there any relationship or not?"

The master said, "As there is perception, there is relationship."

The monk said, "If no other [person] is perceived, what is related to?"

The master said, "If it is not the case [that there is perception], it is your own self."

The monk said, "Can you be perceived or not?"

The master said, "As people move closer, the Way moves farther away."

The monk said, "Why do you hide yourself?"

The master said, "Right now I am openly talking with you."

The monk said, "How can you say you are not moving away?"

The master said, "Because it is obviously so [that I'm moving away]."

The master instructed the assembly saying, "A person that teaches is living in the present life. A person that doesn't teach is living in the third world of karmic retribution.[1] If there is no teaching, all living things will fall [into Hell]. If there is teaching, there is still karmic retribution. Then, will you teach or not?"

A monk said, "I will teach."

The master said, "Are you seen by all living things or not?"

The monk said, "I am unseen."

The master said, "Why are you unseen?"

The monk said, "I have no form."

The master said, "Right now do you see me or not?"

The monk said, "You are not a living thing."

The master said, "If you yourself know the transgression, it[2] is fine."

1   See no. 27.
2   What you say.

121

The master instructed the assembly saying, "The Dragon King's daughter paid her personal homage to the Buddha from her heart. It was a completely natural act."[1]

A monk asked, "If it was natural, why was there any 'paying homage'?"

The master said, "If there was no paying homage, how could it be natural?"

1   See no. 88.

122

The master instructed the assembly saying, "Even if there are eight hundred people who have attained Buddhahood, still it is difficult to find one good Ch'an (Zen) man among them."

123

A monk asked, "Supposing there is a state without Buddhas or people, then is there any practice (left to do) or not?"

The master said, "Even though you completely do away with those two,[1] still there are hundreds, thousands, millions and trillions."[2]

1   Buddhas and people.
2   Of living things to "do away with".

124

A monk asked, "What about it when the white clouds do not fade away?"[1]

The master said, "I don't know anything about meteorology."

The monk said, "Are there no host and guest?"[2]

The master said, "I am host, you are guest. Where are the white clouds?"

1   He is metaphorically speaking about his own enlightenment.
2   See no. 20.

125

A monk asked, "What about it when 'great skill seems like clumsiness'?"[1]

The master said, "The joist and rafter beams have collapsed."

1   The reference is to the Taoist text *Tao Te Ching* by Lao-tzu (Roshi).

126

The master instructed the assembly saying, "I do not enjoy hearing the word 'Buddha'."

A monk asked, "Do you help people or not?"

The master said, "I help people."

The monk said, "How do you help people?"

The master said, "'Not aware of the deep principle, futilely labouring to calm the mind.'"[1]

The monk said, "You said it was deep, but what is the principle?"

The master said, "I don't hold on to a basis."

The monk said, "That is deep, what is the principle?"

The master said, "The principle is answering you."[2]

1   From the *Treatise on Being True to Mind* (*Hsin-hsin-ming*).
2   The act of giving the answer.

127

The master instructed the assembly saying, "Every one of you has Ch'an (Zen) and has the Way. If there is someone who asks you,

'What about Ch'an?' or 'What about the Way?' how will you answer him?"

A monk asked, "Each of us has Ch'an and the Way but, from long ago until now, why has there been so much talk?"

The master said, "Because you are a wandering ghost."[1]

The monk said, "It's not yet clear to me, how do you help people?"[2]

The master retired without saying a word.

1 This type of ghost has no one to do ancestral sacrifices for it, hence it wanders from place to place. The meaning is that there is doubt and lack of confidence in our own nature.

2 "What talk do you have to help wandering ghosts like me?"

128

The master instructed the assembly saying, "To be mindful of Buddha and to be mindful of the Dharma, you cannot be negligent."

A monk asked, "What is being mindful of myself?"

The master said, "Who is it that is being mindful?"

The monk said, "No one else."

The master shouted, "You ass!"

129

The master entered the hall to instruct the assembly and said, "At the first word,[1] you are a teacher for the Patriarchs. At the second word, you are a teacher for the people and heavenly beings. At the third word, you have not even saved yourself."

A monk asked, "What is the first word?"

The master said, "You are a teacher for the Patriarchs."

The master went on saying, "That's really fine to have come right off the top of your head."

The monk again said, "What is the 'first word'?"

The master said, "Now you have gone on to be a teacher for people and heavenly beings."

1   The three words were a formula developed by Lin-chi (Rinzai) and deal with the relationship of form and emptiness, but Chao-chou (Joshu) is not necessarily using them as Lin-chi would.

130

The master said, "It is not that you are not bringing anything forth, nor is it that I am without a response."

A monk asked, "How do you respond?"

The master gave a long sigh.

The monk said, "Haven't you wronged me with this response?"

The master said, "Just now you have acknowledged me, so therefore I have wronged you. If you do not acknowledge me, I will not wrong you."

131

The master instructed the assembly saying, "Tonight I'm going to answer, so somebody come forward and ask a question."

When a monk had come forward to bow the master said, "I threw out a tile hoping to pick up a pearl, but I only got a pot shard."

132

A monk asked, "Does a dog have a Buddha-nature or not?"

The master said, "Not [Mu]!"[1]

The monk said, "Above to all the Buddhas, below to the crawling bugs, all have Buddha-nature. Why is it that the dog has not?"

The master said, "Because he has the nature of karmic delusions."[2]

1   This koan is famous in Zen circles and is known as the "*Mu* koan".

2   "The nature of karmic delusions" is the logical opposite of "Buddha-nature".
    It is the state of mind that is given to the compulsive passions of likes and dis-
    likes based on the thought of separateness.

133

A monk asked, "What is the Dharmakaya?"[1]
The master said, "The Nirmanakaya."[2]
The monk said, "I am not asking about the Nirmanakaya."
The master said, "Just pay attention to the Nirmanakaya."

1   The universal aspect of the three "bodies" of the Buddha.
2   Another of the three "bodies": the material world of changing forms.

134

A monk asked, "What about it when the clear moon is in the sky?"
The master said, "What's your name?"
The monk said, "Me."
The master said, "Where is 'the clear moon in the sky'?"

135

A monk asked "Today is the sixteenth;[1] what about it?"
The master said, "East is east, west is west."
The monk said, "What is 'east is east, west is west'?"
The master said, "Seek but you will not find."

1   It was the sixteenth day of the seventh lunar month, the day when the ninety-
    day summer training period ended and the monks left the temple to travel
    about as they chose.

136

A monk asked, "What about it when I don't understand at all?"
The master said, "I don't understand even more so."

The monk said, "Do you know that or not?"

The master said, "I'm not wooden-headed, what don't I know?"

The monk said, "That's a fine 'not understanding'."

The master clapped his hands and laughed.

137

A monk asked, "What is a person of the Way?"

The master said, "I always say 'a person of Buddha'."

138

A monk said, "Usually, if you say something, raise a hand or move a foot, you have completely fallen into my trap. Please say something that goes beyond [my trap]."

The master said, "I've finished lunch, but not yet had tea."

139

Magistrate Ma (Ba) asked, "Do you do practice or not?"

The master said, "If I did practice I would be in serious difficulty."

The magistrate said, "If you don't do practice, who do you expect to do practice?"

The master said, "You are a person who does practice."

The magistrate said, "Why do you call me a man who does practice?"

The master said, "If you haven't ever practised, how could you have managed to be a servant to the ministers of the king? Has there never been a time when you have been starving and cold and penniless, yet have pulled through?"

The magistrate shed tears and expressed his gratitude.

140

The master instructed the assembly saying, "It is not that you are not bringing forth anything, nor that I am without a response."[1]

Another time he said, "If you don't stand at attention or bow, I won't use my whisk or chair in response."

1   See also no. 130.

141

A monk said, "Where is the place that intellect does not reach?"

The master said, "Come here."

The monk said, "Now that I have come here, it is a place that has been reached. What is a place that thought cannot reach?"

The master held up his hand and said, "What do you call this?"

The monk said, "I call it a hand. What do you call it?"

The master said, "Out of the thousands of names I, too, use that one."

The monk said, "Without reaching for it by any of the thousands of names, right now what do you call it?"

The master said, "In that case, it is the place that intellect does not reach."

The monk bowed.

The master said, "The teachings of Shakyamuni [Buddha] and the teachings of the Patriarchs are your guide [to it]."

The monk said, "The Patriarchs and the Buddhas have been spoken of by the ancients. What is the place that intellect does not reach?"

The master raised one finger and said, "What do you call it?"

The monk was silent.

The master said, "Why don't you speak when knocked on the head?[1] What other doubts do you have?"

1   "Why do you hesitate?"

142

A monk asked, "What is your 'family custom'?"[1]

The master said, "My ears are far away. Speak more loudly."

The monk asked again.

The master said, "You asked about my family custom but I, on the contrary, found out all about your family custom."

1   Your Ch'an (Zen).

143

A monk asked, "What about it when the ten thousand things arise together?"[1]

The master said, "Ten thousand things arise together."

The monk said, "One question and one answer have arisen. What has not arisen?"

The master said, "This chair has not arisen."

While the monk was making his bow the master said, "Do you remember our conversation?"

The monk said, "Yes."

The master said, "Try to repeat it."

Whatever the monk tried to say the master refuted.[2]

1   The monk is asking about the interdependent coming-into-being of material forms.

2   This part is not clear in the text.

144

A monk asked, "What is the Buddha right before my eyes?"

The master said, "The one inside the Buddha Hall is."[1]

The monk said, "That is an image of Buddha. What is Buddha?"

The master said, "Mind is."

The monk said, "Mind is still something limited. What is Buddha?"

The master said, "Not mind is."

The monk said, "Mind or not mind, do you allow me to choose between them?"

The master said, "Mind or not mind, you can choose as you wish, and, if you can, tell me which one it is and it will be all right."

1 Chao-chou (Joshu) is referring to the statue in the Buddha Hall.

145

A monk asked, "I've come a long way to see you; it's not clear to me, what is your 'family custom'?"

The master said, "I don't talk about it to people."

The monk said, "Why do you not talk about it to people?"

The master said, "That's my family custom."

The monk said, "You do not talk about it, but why do the four seas[1] come to see you?"

The master said, "You are the sea, I am not the sea."

The monk said, "It's not clear to me, what is in the sea?"

The master said "I've hooked one!"

1 People in the world of birth and death.

146

A monk asked, "What sort of person is it that doesn't associate with the Buddhas?"

The master said, "He is not a Buddha."

The monk said, "How come he doesn't associate with them?"

The master said, "If I tell you it is not Buddha, not a living thing, not an object, is that enough?"

The monk said, "What is it?"

The master said, "If it is named, it is either Buddha or a living thing."

The monk said, "Can't it simply be just as it is?"

The master said, "In the end, I can't go along with you."[1]

1   "The idea is good but ..."

147

A monk asked, "What is 'ordinary mind'?"
The master said, "Foxes, wolves, and jackals."

148

A monk asked, "By what means is 'hearing without hearing' accomplished?"
The master said, "Setting aside not hearing, what do you hear?"

149

A monk asked, "I've heard that in your teaching there is a saying about the Mani Jewel.[1] What is its original colour?"
The master called out the monk's name.
The monk said, "Yes?"
The master said, "Come here."
The monk came forward and asked again, "What is its original colour?"
The master said, "Only reflected colour!"[2]

1   The Mani Jewel reflects all colours but itself has no colour.
2   This is as much a scolding of the monk as an answer.

150

A monk asked, "Can a person of 'ordinary mind' be taught or not?"
The master said, "I don't pass through his front door."
The monk said, "In that case, hasn't that person sunk completely into the 'other side'?"[1]
The master said, "A fine 'ordinary mind' that is!"[2]

1   Nirvana, or enlightenment.
2   Chao-chou (Joshu) is scolding the monk.

151

A monk asked, "What is the fact that I accept responsibility for?"
   The master said, "To the ends of time you'll never single it out."

152

A monk said, "Who is a person of 'great practice'?"
   The master said, "The head monk of this temple is."

153

A monk asked, "I have just come here and know nothing. What are my duties?"
   The master said, "What's your name?"
   The monk said, "Hui-han (Enan)."
   The master said, "A fine 'knowing nothing' that is."

154

A monk asked, "I am striving to learn, but that is to slander you. How can I not slander you?"
   The master said, "What's your name?"
   The monk said, "Tao-chiao."
   The master said, "Go to a quiet place, you rice bag."

155

A monk asked, "What is your 'great mind'?"
The master said, "It's neither big nor small."
The monk said, "That's your 'great mind', isn't it?"
The master said, "If there's even one hair's breadth [of thought

about it, such as that], for ten thousand *kalpas*[1] it would not be so."

1   A *kalpa* is the longest unit of time measurement in Buddhist philosophy. "Ten thousand kalpas" means "for ever".

156

A monk asked, "'The ten thousand dharmas are originally tranquil, yet man himself jumbles them up.'[1] Who said this?"

The master said, "If he comes forth he will die."

1   It is not clear whether these words were spoken by Nan-yang Hui-chung (Nan-yo Echu, d. 776) or were from his memorial stone.

157

A monk said, "'It is not Buddha, not a living thing, not an object';[1] this cuts off speech. What does not cut off speech?"

The master said, "'Heaven above and Earth below, only I alone am honoured.'"[2]

1   See also no. 146.
2   The words said to have been spoken by Shakyamuni Buddha when he was born.

158

A monk asked, "What is the perfect circle of Vairocana?"[1]

The master said, "From the time I left home when I was young, I have had no hallucinations."

The monk said, "Do you help people or not?"

The master said, "I pray that you for ever look upon the perfect circle of Vairocana."

1   Vairocana Buddha or "Great Iluminator Buddha" is the Dharmakaya, pure and universal essence, of the Buddha as expounded in the *Avatamsaka Sutra*. The "perfect circle of Vairocana" means the essential reality of the universe

(Dharmakaya) manifest in its myriad phenomena (Nirmanakaya)

159

A monk asked, "In the days of the Buddha, it was transmitted by the Buddha. After Buddha passed into nirvana, who is there to transmit it?"

The master said, "The entirety of the past and present are in me."

The monk said, "It's not clear to me, what was it that was transmitted?"

The master said, "All things are subject to birth and death."

The monk said, "It's impossible to do away entirely with the Buddhas and Patriarchs?"

The master said, "What was it that was transmitted?"

160

A monk asked, "What about it when both ordinary and holy do not exist?"

The master said, "I pray that you become a great saint. I am someone who is a hindrance to the Buddhas and Patriarchs."

161

A monk asked, "The name of Chao-chou (Joshu) is heard far and wide, why is it that he cannot be seen?"

The master said, "It's my fault."

162

A monk asked, "The clear moon is in the sky. It is not clear to me, what about the fact within the room?"[1]

The master said, "Ever since I left home, I have done nothing to earn a living."

The monk said, "In that case, you do not help the people of the world."

The master said, "I cannot save myself from my own ills; how could I save others from their ills?"

The monk said, "If you deal with my independence?"[2]

The master said, "If you are dependent, you walk on the ground. If you are not dependent, you can do with east and west as you please."

1 In other words, "What is it to be a Ch'an (Zen) teacher?"
2 Be without the help of others.

163

A monk asked, "What about it when the mind is not perceived by the mind [itself]?"

The master said, "Who is perceived?"

The monk said, "The self is perceived."

The master said, "There are not two [selves]."

164

A monk asked, "What about it when 'external form is disregarded'?"[1]

The master pointed to a water bottle and said, "What's that?"

The monk said, "A water bottle."

The master said, "A fine 'disregarding external form' that is."

1 From the *Treatise on Being True to Mind* (*Hsin-hsin ming*): "The smallest is at once big; completely forget about the world. The biggest is at once small; disregard external form."

165

A monk asked, "What is 'returning to the root?'"[1]

The master said, "To seek [for it] is to deviate [from it]."[2]

1 From the *Treatise on Being True to Mind*: "Returning to the root, the essence

is realized. Following appearance, the foundation is lost."

2   See also no. 1.

166

A monk asked, "Without separating from words, how can self-liberation be accomplished?"

The master said, "Separating from words is self-liberation."

The monk said, "A moment ago no one made me come here."

The master said, "Why did you come here?"

The monk said, "Why don't you try to bring it[1] forth?"

The master said, "I just did."

1   "The reason I came here."

167

A monk asked, "Without the mind, there is no knowledge. Please give me one word [about this]."

The master said, "I can't keep up with you."[1]

1   "You're too smart for me."

168

A monk asked, "What is the resolution?"[1]

The master said, "The resolution."

The monk said, "What is it the resolution of?"

The master said, "I am the resolution. You don't know what you're asking about."

The monk said, "It's not that I haven't asked about anything."

The master said, "Where is the resolution of that?"

1   The usual grammatical understanding of the characters used here is the summary or decision of an issue that has been discussed back and forth.

169

A monk asked, "What about it when I'm not wearing a stitch of clothing?"

The master said, "What are you not wearing?"

The monk said, "I'm not wearing a stitch of clothing."

The master said, "A fine 'not wearing a stitch of clothing' that is."

170

A monk asked, "What is 'like a man trying to save his head that is on fire'?"

The master said, "Study."

The monk said, "Where?"

The master said, "Don't stand in someone else's place."

171

A monk asked, "In the kalpa of emptiness,[1] who is the master?"

The master said, "I'm sitting right here."

The monk said, "What Dharma are you talking about?"

The master said, "I'm talking about what you're asking about."

1   There are four kalpas, or ages, in Buddhist philosophy; the kalpa of becoming, the kalpa of dwelling, the kalpa of destruction and the kalpa of emptiness.

172

A monk asked, "I've heard that long ago there was a saying, 'The empty radiance illumines itself'.[1] What is [the meaning of] 'illumines itself'?"

The master said, "Don't talk about the illumination of something else."

The monk said, "What about the place where illumination doesn't reach?"

The master said, "You've talked it to death."

1   The source is unknown.

173

A monk asked, "What was *it* itself?"

The master said, "The time when a thought does not arise."

174

A monk asked, "What is the Dharma King?"

The master said, "The king of this province is."

The monk said, "You aren't."

The master said, "You are seeking to rebel without ever realizing who the king is."

175

A monk asked, "What is 'Buddha-mind'?"

The master said, "You are mind, I am Buddha. Whether to attend upon me or not, you must see for yourself."

The monk said, "You are not lacking it, so shouldn't you be attended upon?"

The master said, "You teach me."

176

A monk asked, "Among the three bodies[1] which is the original body?"

The master said, "It is impossible to take away any one of them."

1   Dharmakaya, Sambhogakaya, Nirmanakaya. The three aspects of the Bud-dhakaya or Buddha "body": universal and essential truth, psychological experience and myriad physical forms. See no. 113.

A monk asked, "It's not yet clear to me, who is the Patriarch of this land?"

The master said, "Bodhidharma has come, so here we are all patriarchs."[1]

The monk said, "What number generation are you [in descent from Bodhidharma]?"

The master said, "I do not fall into any position."[2]

The monk said, "Where are you?"

The master said, "Inside your ears."

1   A statement of Bodhidharma's teaching.
2   Another statement of Bodhidharma's teaching.

A monk asked, "It is said, 'Do not abandon the root, do not chase after phenomena'.[1] What is the True Way?"

The master said, "A fine 'monk that has left home' you are."

The monk said, "In the past I never did leave home."

The master said, "I take shelter in the Buddha, I take shelter in the Dharma."[2]

The monk said, "It's not clear to me; is there a home that can be left or not?"

The master said, "Just leave home."

The monk asked, "Where does the person who has left home settle down?"

The master said, "Sitting quietly at home."

1   The source of the reference is unknown.
2   This stanza is chanted at the ordination ceremony.

A monk asked, "'A clear-eyed person sees everything.'[1] Then do they see forms or not?"

The master said, "They are smashed completely."

The monk said, "How are they smashed?"

The master said, "Force is not used."

The monk said, "If force is not used, how are they smashed?"

The master said, "If force is used, they have deviated."[2]

1 The source of the quotation is unknown.
2 They have deviated from being a clear-eyed person.

180

A monk asked, "Whom does the great mind of Buddha help?"

The master said, "It helps only the present."

The monk said, "How come they are not able to deal with it?"

The master said, "Whose fault is that?"

The monk said, "How is it to be grasped?"

The master said, "Right now there is no one who grasps it."

The monk said, "In that case, there is nothing that can be relied upon."

The master said, "However, you cannot do without me."

181

A monk asked, "What is a person who understands matters perfectly?"

The master said, "Obviously it is great practice."

The monk said, "It's not yet clear to me; do you practise or not?"

The master said, "I wear clothes and eat food."

The monk said, "Wearing clothes and eating food are ordinary things. It's still not clear to me; do you practise or not?"

The master said, "You tell me, what am I doing every day?"

Doctor Ts'ui (Sai Rochu) asked, "Does an accomplished person[1] go to Hell or not?"

The master said, "I entered at the head of the line."

Sai Rochu said, "You are an accomplished person, why do you go to Hell?"

The master said, "If I had not gone, how could I have met you?"

1   See no. 13 for full explanation of this phrase.

183

A monk asked, "What about it when there is a hair's breadth of differentiation?"

The master said, "Heaven and Earth are far removed from each other."

The monk said, "What about it when there is not a hair's breadth of differentiation?"

The master said, "Heaven and Earth are far removed from each other."

184

A monk asked, "What is 'the eye that does not sleep'?"[1]

The master said, "The common eye[2] and the bodily eye."

The master added, "Even though the heavenly eye is not attained, the strength of the bodily eye is such."

The monk said, "What is the eye that sleeps?"

The master said, "The Buddha eye and the Dharma eye are the eyes that sleep."

1   In the *Treatise on Being True to Mind* (*Hsin-hsin Ming*) it is said: "If the eyes do not sleep, all dreams vanish naturally."

2   In Buddhist philosophy, there are five kinds of eyes: bodily eyes, heavenly eyes, wisdom eyes, Dharma eyes, Buddha eyes. The "common eyes" are Chao-chou's (Joshu's) own addition and are to be seen on a par with "bodily eyes".

A monk asked, "Having chased him all the way to Mount T'a-sou (Daiyu), why didn't he pick them up?"[1]

The master picked up the hem of his robe and said, "Where can you get this?"

The monk said, "I'm not asking about this one."

The master said, "In that case, you can't pick it up."

1   The monk is referring to the famous story about Ming Shan-tso (Myo Joza) and the Sixth Patriarch Hui-neng (Eno). Ming Shan-tso caught up with the Sixth Patriarch at Mount T'a-sou and there the scene of enlightenment, recorded in case twenty-three of the *Mumonkan* (*Wu-men Kuan*), takes place.

186

A monk asked, "Without uniting it or breaking it up, how is it known about?"

The master said, "You are one, I am one."

The monk said, "That is uniting, what is separating?"

The master said, "You are doing the uniting."

187

A monk asked, "What is the unmistaken path?"

The master said, "Awakening to your mind, seeing your nature; these are the unmistaken path."

188

A monk asked, "The bright jewel[1] is in my hand. Is there anything that is illuminated or not?"

The master said, "Illumination is not lacking, but what are you calling a 'jewel'?"

1   Enlightenment.

189

A monk asked, "What about it when the 'mystic sprout' has no root?"[1]

The master said, "Where have you come from?"

The monk said, "From the town of Ta-yuan."

The master said, "A fine 'no root' that is."

1   The monk is referring to himself as a free and independent enlightened person.

190

A monk asked, "What about it when I seek to be Buddha?"

The master said, "What a tremendous waste of energy."

The monk said, "What about it when I'm not wasting any energy?"

The master said, "In that case, you are Buddha."

191

A monk asked, "I am chaotically adrift and drowning; how can I get out of it?"

The master just sat motionless.

The monk said, "I'm asking you sincerely."

The master said, "Where are you 'adrift and drowning'?"

192

A monk asked, "It is neither ordinary nor holy. How can you escape going to these two?"

The master said, "I answer you removed from both of them."

The monk said, "Thank you."

The master said, "From where does that 'thank you' arise? Right here, it arose from me. When you are in town, from where does it arise?"

The monk said, "Why don't you decide it?"

The master said, "I will teach you. Why don't you say, 'Today there's a nice breeze'?"

193

A monk asked, "What is a person who is a great *icchantika*?"[1]

The master said, "I am answering you. Do you believe it or not?"

The monk said, "Your words are weighty, how dare I not believe them?"

The master said, "I sought for the icchantika, but he's hard to find."

1 An icchantika is a person who has absolutely no good in them and who is unable to believe anything. It means someone who is lacking in Buddha-nature.

194

A monk asked, "Where can a person who is wholly without shame be found?"

The master said, "He can't be found here."

The monk said, "What if he should suddenly show up?"

The master said, "Get him out of here!"

195

A monk asked, "What about it when action is not manifest?"[1]

The master said, "It is not that there is no action, but who is manifesting it?"

1 The monk is asking about the "action that leaves no traces".

196

A monk asked, "In the kalpa (age) of emptiness,[1] is there anyone who does practice or not?"

The master said, "What are you calling 'the kalpa of emptiness'?"

The monk said, "There is not even one thing."

The master said, "That is where you can say practice starts. What are you calling 'the kalpa of emptiness'?"

1   See no. 171 for explanation of this phrase.

197

A monk asked, "What is 'leaving home'?"

The master said, "Not aspiring to acclaim, not seeking after defilements."

198

A monk asked, "Without pointing to a Dharma, what is your Dharma?"

The master said, "I don't expound the Dharma of the Taoists."

The monk said, "You don't expound the Dharma of the Taoists, but what is your Dharma?"

The master said, "I told you, I don't expound the Dharma of the Taoists."

The monk said, "That's it, isn't it?"

The master said, "I've never used that¹ to instruct people."

1   That statement.

199

A monk asked, "What is the one path of self-liberation that is right before my eyes?"

The master said, "'Not two, not three.'"¹

The monk said, "The path is right before my eyes, then am I permitted to advance upon it or not?"

The master said, "In that case, [you can advance for] a thousand or ten thousand miles."

1   The reference is to the *Saddharma Pundarika Sutra* in which it is said that there is just one vehicle to enlightenment, not two or three.

200

A monk asked, "What is the fact that goes beyond Vairocana?"[1]

The master said, "I am under your feet."

The monk said, "Why are you under my feet?"

The master said "From the outset, you didn't know that there was a fact that went beyond."

1   The "Great Iluminator Buddha" associated with the pure or absolute essence (Dharmakaya) of the Buddha. See also no. 158.

201

A monk asked "What is it to be at one?"

The master said, "You are not at one."

The monk said, "What is to be 'not at one'?"

The master said, "Look at what was just said."

202

A monk asked, "What is your mind itself?"

The master said, "Stop! Stop! 'The subtlety of my Dharma is hard to conceive.'"[1]

1   These words are borrowed from the *Saddharma Pundarika Sutra*.

203

A monk said, "What about it when there is absolute purity without any blemishes?"

The master said, "Flung into pits, thrown into holes."

The monk said, "Where is the error?"

The master said, "You have wronged the person who is just like that."[1]

1   The one who is pure and without blemishes.

204

A monk asked, "It is not yet clear to me, what about it when someone vows to leave home and search for Supreme Wisdom?"

The master said, "If you have not left home, wisdom uses you;
after leaving home you can use wisdom."

205

There was a scholar who saw the staff in the master's hand and
said, "The Buddha never denied the prayers and requests of any
living thing. Is that not so?"

The master said, "It is so."

The scholar said, "Then I beg to have that staff in your hand. Is
that all right?"

The master said, "A gentleman[1] does not deny people their finest
things."

The scholar said, "I am not a gentleman."

The master said, "I, likewise, am not a Buddha."

1   The term for the ideal man of the Confucianists.

206

The master once went out and saw an old woman seeding a field.
The master said, "What do you do when a ferocious tiger comes?"

The old woman said, "There is not one dharma that can be
applied."

[The old woman turned back to her work and] the master
shouted, "WAA!"

The old woman screamed, "WAA!"

The master said, "You still have that [dharma to use]."

There was a scholar who was taking leave of the master who said, "I have been here a long while being a nuisance to you, but I have not been able to reply to any of your questions. Some day I will come back here as a donkey and give a proper reply to you."

The master said, "How will you make me get in the saddle?"

208

When the master went to Tao-wu's (Dogo's)[1] place, he had just entered the monk's hall when Tao-wu said, "One arrow from Nan-ch'uan (Nansen) has come."

The master said, "Look, the arrow!"

Tao-wu said, "Missed!"

The master said, "Bull's-eye!"

1   Tao-wu yuan-chih (Dogo Enchi, 769–835) was a disciple of Yueh-shan (Yaku-san) and a Dharma brother of Yun-yen T'an-sheng (Ungan Donjo). The words "Look, the arrow!" were famous words of Yueh-shan and the meaning was undoubtedly well known to both men prior to their meeting.

PART TWO

Questions & Answers

209

The master entered the hall and instructed the assembly saying, "Metal Buddhas can't pass through a furnace, wood Buddhas can't pass through fire, mud Buddhas can't pass through water. The true Buddha sits within you. Bodhi,[1] nirvana, suchness, and Buddha-nature, are just clothes stuck on the body, and, as such, are to be called compulsive passions. If you do not ask about them, they are not compulsive passions. Where can the True Realm of Reality be found?

"'If you do not give birth to the mind, the ten thousand dharmas are not transgressed.'[2] Just sit and go into [this matter] for twenty or thirty years. If you do not come to an understanding, you can cut off my head.

"'Dreams and hallucinations, it is wasted labour to try and hold on to them.'[3] 'If you do not diverge from mind, the ten thousand dharmas are naturally so.'[4] It can not be obtained from outside, so what else is there to be related to? It is just like a goat, other than haphazardly picking up things in his mouth and eating them, what does he do?

"When I met Yueh-shan (Yakusan),[5] he said, 'If there is someone who questions me, all I do is shut his *yap*[6] for him.' I also say, 'Shut your yap'.

"'To hold on to self is corrupt, to not hold on to self is pure.'[7] It is just like a mad dog who is always trying to get more and more to eat. Where is the Buddha to be found? Thousands and ten thousands of people are 'seeking-for-Buddha' fools. If you try to find one person of the Way [among them] there are none. If you want to become a disciple of the 'King of Emptiness',[8] don't give illness to your mind.[9]

"When the world was not, there was still this reality. When the world is destroyed, this reality is not destroyed. Take one look at me, I am nothing other than I am. The True Self is simply this. Right here what more is there to be sought for? At such a time, don't turn your head away or change your expression. If you do so, it is immediately lost."

1   Transcendental Wisdom.
2   From the *Treatise on Being True to Mind* (*Hsin-hsin ming*).
3   *Ibid.*
4   *Ibid.*
5   Yueh-shan Wei-yen (Yakusan Igen, 751–828 CE) was a disciple of Shih-t'ou (Sekito) and one of the great Ch'an (Zen) masters of the middle T'ang. As the grandfather of Tung-shan (Tozan), he is one of the Patriarchs of the Ts'ao-tung (Soto) sect of Ch'an (Zen).
6   Literally "dog mouth".
7   From the *Vimalikirti-nirdesa Sutra*.
8   The True Self.
9   From the *Treatise on Being True to Mind*.

210

A monk asked, "What about it when all the bones are pulverized and there is one everlasting spirit?"

The master said, "It's windy again this morning."

211

A monk asked, "I'm not asking about the three vehicles or the twelve-part teaching.[1] What is the mind that the Patriarch brought from the west?"[2]

The master said, "An ox is giving birth to a calf.[3] Take a look at it."

The monk said, "I don't understand, what is the meaning of that?"

The master said, "I don't know either."

1   See no. 78.
2   See no. 12.
3   This was probably an actual event happening that day at the temple.

212

A monk asked, "What about when the ten thousand nations[1] come to the imperial palace?"

The master said, "Meeting someone but not calling out his name."

1   The whole world.

213

A monk asked, "During the twelve parts of the day,[1] how is the washing[2] to be done?"

The master said, "Quickly swept along to the west in the muddy waters of the river of Hell."

The monk said, "Will Manjushri[3] be seen there or not?"

The master said, "You blockhead! Where have you gone to?"

1   The Chinese system of time divides the day into twelve two-hour periods.
2   The words mean "to wash rice", "to separate the gravel from the grain", a metaphor for purifying the mind.
3   The reference is to the *Avatamsaka Sutra* where the aspirant searches for a wise man and the last one is met by crossing the river of Hell. The last wise man was Manjushri, the bodhisattva or demi-god who embodies the wisdom of non-dualistic mind.

214

A monk asked, "What is the 'practice hall'?"[1]

The master said, "From the practice hall you have come. From the practice hall you will go. Everything [everywhere] is the practice hall. There is no other place."

1 "Practice hall" literally means "Way place" or "place to practise the Way". In the *Vimalikirti-nirdesa Sutra*, Vimalikirti is asked by a bodhisattva, "Where have you come from?" Vimalikirti answers, "From the practice hall." The bodhisattva asks further, "What sort of place is the practice hall?" Vimalikirti answers, "Mind itself is the practice hall."

215

A monk asked, "What about it when no blossoms have yet appeared?"

The master said, "If their fragrance is smelt, your brains fall out."

The monk said, "What about it when the fragrance is not smelt?"

The master said, "I don't have time to waste like that."

216

A monk asked, "What is multiplicity?"

The master said, "One, two, three, four, five."

The monk said, "What is the fact of the state of not relating to multiplicity?"

The master said, "One, two, three, four, five."

217

A monk asked, "What is the world in which there is no day and night?"

The master said, "Right now, is it day or night?"

The monk said, "I'm not asking about right now."

The master said, "How can you deal with me?"

A monk asked, "The robe of Venerable Kasyapa[1] has not trodden down the Ts'ao-ch'i (Sokei) road.[2] Who is able to wear it?"

The master said, "The sky does not 'go into the world'.[3] People of the Way don't know anything about it."[4]

1 Kasyapa was the successor of Shakyamuni Buddha.
2 According to Ch'an (Zen) tradition the robe and bowl, symbols of the line of succession from Shakyamuni, were brought to China by Bodhidharma and eventually were transmitted to the Sixth Patriarch, Ts'ao-ch'i Hui-neng (Sokei Eno). There was a story, however, that Kasyapa never died and was hiding at Vulture Peak to await the arrival of Maitreya (the future Buddha), to transmit them to him. So the monk is suggesting that the Ch'an Dharma transmission is a dubious matter.
3 The words used are those when a monk "goes out into the world" to teach.
4 They know nothing about the wearing of the "robe".

219

A monk asked, "What is mixing, yet not becoming confused?"
The master said, "I have fasted as a vegetarian for a long time."
The monk said, "Are you able to transcend it or not?"
The master said, "The fast would be broken."

220

A monk asked, "What are the words of the ancients?"
The master said, "Listen carefully! Listen carefully!"

221

A monk asked, "What is the fact of my own nature?"
The master said, "If you put it that way, is there anything you dislike?"

222

A monk asked, "The ten thousand dharmas return to the One. Where does the One return to?"

The master said, "When I was in Ch'ing-chou[1] I made a hempen robe. It weighed seven pounds."

1   An area in eastern Shantung.

223

A monk asked, "What is a child that leaves home?"

The master said, "He does not salute the emperor but, on the contrary, bows to his parents."

224

A monk asked, "What about the fact that is right in front of my eyes?"

The master said, "You're a person that is right before my eyes."

225

A monk asked, "What sort of person is it that goes beyond Buddha?"

The master said, "Anyone who is leading an ox and ploughing the fields."

226

A monk asked, "What is 'fast'?"

The master said, "If I told you what it was, what would you do about it?"

The monk said, "I don't understand."

The master said, "I say to you, 'If you quickly put on your shoes and go stand in the water, a galloping horse would arrive at Chan-An (Choan)[1] before the shoes got wet'."

1 The ancient capital of China.

227

A monk asked, "What about when the four mountains[1] close in upon each other?"

The master said, "Where no road is, Chao-chou (Joshu) is."

1 The "four mountains" could be either the mountains of the four directions, or birth, old age, sickness and death.

228

A monk asked, "What about it when the ancient palace is without a king?"[1]

The master coughed.

The monk said, "In that case, I'm addressing Your Majesty."

The master said, "The body of the thief has been exposed."

1 There is sameness without any differentiation.

229

A monk asked, "How old are you?"

The master said, "You can never finish counting the beads of the *juzu*."[1]

1 A *juzu* is a string of beads like a rosary which Buddhist priests carry. It has one hundred and eight beads on a circular string.

230

A monk asked, "Who is a man of your line?"[1]

The master said, "Ts'ung-shen (Jushin)."[2]

1   Dharma line; line of succession.

2   Ts'ung-shen was Chao-chou's (Joshu's) own name.

231

A monk asked, "While I am travelling around, if someone asks me, 'What Dharma does Chao-chou (Joshu) expound?', what should I reply?"

The master said, "Salt is expensive, rice is cheap."[1]

1   In the days of the T'ang dynasty salt was a government monopoly and very expensive; rice was common and quite cheap.

232

A monk asked, "What is Buddha?"

The master said, "Aren't you Buddha?"

233

A monk asked, "What is 'leaving home'?"

The master said, "How have you managed to meet me?"

234

A monk asked, "What is that which is continued from the Buddhas to the Patriarchs?"

The master said, "Nothing has leaked away."

235

A monk asked, "Please point to the foundation for me."

The master said, "The foundation is without illness."

The monk said, "What is the realization of it?"

The master said, "He who has realized it knows."

The monk said, "Then what is that experience?"

The master said, "You put a name on it for me."

236

A monk asked, "What about it when the Pure One is unadulterated?"

The master said, "A fine question that is."

237

A monk asked, "Doesn't a person of quietude and non-action settle into the deep void?"[1]

The master said, "He is settled into the deep void."

The master said, "What is the resolution of it?"

The master said, "Being donkeys and horses."

1   The "deep void" here is a reference to the "seventh world of difficulty" for the bodhisattva, where there is the desire simply to contemplate the formless and not come out into the world.

238

A monk asked, "What is the mind that the Patriarch brought from the west?"

The master said, "This chair leg is."

The monk said, "That's it, isn't it?"

The master said, "If it is, take it away with you."

239

A monk asked, "What about when there is absolute purity without any blemish?"[1]

The master said, "I am right here, don't make me into a common servant."

1   See also no. 203.

240

A monk asked, "What about when a flying peacock has not yet arrived?"[1]

The master said, "From where did it take to the air?"

1   The monk is speaking of himself as not yet having enlightenment.

241

A monk asked, "What about when the True Realm of Reality has no dust upon it?"[1]

The master said, "Everything is right here."

1   See also no. 116.

242

A monk asked, "What is the one word?"[1]

The master said, "Yes?"

The monk said, "What is the one word?"

The master said, "I'm not deaf."

1   See also no. 25.

243

A monk asked, "Is a baby that is just being born endowed with the six consciousnesses[1] or not?"

The master said, "A ball thrown into a rushing stream."

1   The six consciousnesses are the five senses and thought.

A monk asked, "What about it when each and every thing has been brought here?"

The master said, "That is still a hundred paces away from me."[1]

1   In other words, "You're still discriminating".

A monk asked, "What is your 'family custom'?"

The master said, "Since the time I left home as a young man, I have lived as an ascetic[1] and never worked for a living."

1   A life according to the twelve *dhutas* or ascetic rules.

A monk asked, "I ask you to say something apart from the four statements."[1]

The master said, "I am always here."

1   The four statements are "is", "is not", "both is and is not", "neither is nor is not".

A monk asked, "Why does Doctor P'ien-ch'ueh[1] have illness?"

The master said, "Pien-ch'ueh is not separate from the bed and pillow [of the sick bed]."

Again he said, "One drop of sweet dew[2] moistens the Great Thousand[3] everywhere."

1   P'ien-ch'ueh was one of the two great doctors of ancient China who was able to bring the dead to life.
2   Enlightenment.
3   A metaphor for the infinite number of worlds in the universe.

A monk asked, "What is the white ox in the open ground?"[1]

The master said, "You dumb ox!"

1 See also no. 85.

A monk asked, "What is the form of a great man?"

The master looked around the hall.[1]

The monk said, "Even so, this is still leaving your position and scurrying about in attendance."[2]

The master said, "I don't have time to waste running around for such a good-for-nothing [as you]."

1 Looking at the people in the hall, at everyone but the monk.
2 The words used are those used for the servants or lesser officials who, as a matter of politeness, scurry around in attendance on greater officials and lords. The monk is saying that that action itself is in effect giving recognition.

A monk asked, "If there is even a little intellectual thinking, it falls into the world of humans or the world of heavenly beings.[1] What about when close rapport is settled into unintentionally?"[2]

The master said, "Not just me, but good Ch'an (Zen) people too have no answer for you."

1 The highest two of the six realms of existence.
2 Wu-hsin (Japanese mu shin), lit. "no mind". The monk uses this Ch'an jargon here so that it also has a non-jargon meaning which I have translated as "unintentionally".

A monk asked, "Always 'action having a purpose'[1] will finally settle to the bottom as dregs and scum. Please reply without an 'action having a purpose'."

The master shouted at a nun,[2] "Get some water and clean out the kettle!"

1　The word is a technical term being roughly equal to the Sanskrit word *san-sjruta*, meaning actions that are involved in the world of cause and effect.
2　Evidently nuns also lived at Chao-chou's (Joshu's) temple.

252

A monk asked, "What is the Great Perfection of Wisdom?"[1]
The master said, "Great Perfection of Wisdom."

1　*Maha Prajna-paramita.*

253

A monk asked, "What is a 'man-eating lion'?"
The master said, "I take shelter in Buddha, I take shelter in the Dharma, I take shelter in the sangha![1] Don't eat me."

1　Chanted at the ordination ceremony. See also no. 178.

254

A monk asked, "Apart from words, please say something."
The master coughed.

255

A monk asked, "How can you not slander the ancients and be faithful to them at the same time?"
The master said, "What are you doing?"

256

A monk asked, "What is the one word?"[1]

The master said, "Say something."

1   See also no. 25.

257

A monk asked, "What is one word?"
The master said, "Two words."

258

A monk asked, "It is said that Buddha alone is an accomplished person,[1] what about that?"
The master said, "Heresy."

1   See no. 13.

259

A monk asked, "What is a bodhisattva?"[1]
The master said, "Right here is an icchantika."[2]

1   A bodhisattva is a person who has delayed nirvana to work for the salvation of others.
2   See no. 193. Chao-chou (Joshu) is referring to the monk.

260

A monk asked, "What is the form of a great man?"[1]
The master said, "You're a good boy."

1   See also no. 249.

261

A monk asked, "What about it when there is complete serenity independent of anything?"

The master said, "I am right behind you."[1]

1   In other words, "I'm depending on you."

262

A monk asked, "What is the sangha?"
  The master said, "What else is there but it?"
  The monk said, "What is a person of the sangha?"
  The master said, "Me and you."

263

A monk asked, "Two dragons are fighting for a pearl. Which one gets it?"[1]
  The master said, "I'm just watching."

1   "How do you go beyond duality?"

264

A monk asked, "What is a person who is removed from cause and effect?"
  The master said, "There is no cause for your question, and I am completely oblivious to it."

265

A monk asked, "The many blind men felt the elephant and each one spoke about a different part of it.[1] What is the true elephant?"
  The master said, "There is nothing unreal, of itself it [the elephant] is unknown."

1   The reference is to the *Nirvana Sutra* in which blind men feel an elephant and describe what it is like. Each man feels a different part, so naturally their descriptions vary. The man who feels the trunk thinks it is a snake, the man who feels the leg thinks it is a tree and so on.

A monk asked, "What is the one word?"[1]
The master coughed.
The monk said, "That's it, isn't it?"
The master said, "I can't even cough."[2]

1 See no. 25.
2 "I can't even cough without it being interpreted."

A monk asked, "Does the Great Ocean receive the myriad streams or not?"
The master said, "The Great Sea says, 'I don't know'."
The monk said, "Why doesn't it know?"
The master said, "Finally, it can't say, 'I receive the myriad streams'."

A monk asked, "Who is the teacher of Vairocana?"[1]
The master said, "Vairocana! Vairocana!"

1 See no. 158.

A monk asked, "Have all the Buddhas had a teacher or not?"
The master said, "They have."
The monk said, "What is the teacher of all the Buddhas?"
The master said, "Amitabha Buddha! Amitabha Buddha!"[1]

1 According to Buddhist scriptures, Amitabha Buddha is the Buddha in the Western Heaven who sees all living things. There is a teaching, still very popular in Japan today, that to invoke the name of Amitabha (Amida) will ensure rebirth in the Western Heaven. The Western Heaven is also called "the Pure Land".

270

A monk asked, "What is my teacher?"

The master said, "Clouds rising out of the mountains, streams entering the valley without a sound."

The monk said, "I didn't ask about them."

The master said, "Though they are your teacher, you don't recognize them."

271

A monk asked, "Everywhere [people] just speak with their mouths. How do you instruct people?"

The master kicked over the censer with his foot and pointed to it.

The monk said, "That's it, isn't it?"

The master said, "You got a good look at my foot."

272

A monk asked, "What about when the Great Way is not followed?"

The master said, "You salt peddler!"[1]

The monk said, "What about when the Great Way is followed?"

The master said, "Give me back my passport."[2]

1 In China during the T'ang dynasty, salt was a government monopoly and the price was very high. The people who were salt dealers were naturally disliked by the people.

2 In T'ang China papers were needed to travel about since the government kept a close watch on the movements of the people.

273

A monk asked, "What is the original body?"

The master said, "Once you have come to know me, I am nothing other than that fellow who you met."

The monk said, "If that's the case, you have a life that's separate from other things."

The master said, "Not just this life, but in a thousand of ten thousand lives you will not come to know me."

274

A monk asked, "What is the mind that the Patriarch brought from the west?"

The master said, "How long have the reed flowers been on the east wall?"

275

A monk asked, "What about when there is neither a square nor a circle?"

The master said, "Neither square nor circle."

The monk said, "When things are like that, what about it?"

The master said, "Either square or circle."

276

A monk asked, "What about when people of the Way meet each other?"

The master said, "Bring out the lacquer bowls."[1]

1 Lacquer bowls are used to serve guests at special occasions.

277

A monk asked, "Why can't the Truth be contemplated?'

The master said, "It is not that there is no Truth, only that it is impossible to contemplate it."

The monk said, "What is the resolution of it?"

The master said, "The Truth is forgotten."

278

A monk asked, "What about it when practice has no end and enquiry has no end?'

The master said, "Whether there is an end or not, in the eyes of a person of the Way it is like a drop of spit."

The monk said, "What is the fact of 'that' [state of mind]?"

The master spat on the ground.

279

A monk asked, "What is the mind that the Patriarch brought from the west?"

The master said, "If you don't call it the 'Patriarch's mind', it would be even more so."

The monk said, "What is the original thing?"[1]

The master said, "Four eyes are looking at each other. Outside of this, there is not a second controlling power."[2]

1   "What is the fundamental reality?"
2   The characters translated as "controlling power" refer to a master or lord who is in control of something. The reference is to the idea of a "True Self".

280

A monk asked, "Neither a form nor a manner is maintained, then can you understand or not?"

The master said, "The present moment, do you understand it?"

281

A monk asked, "What is a person who is wholly without shame?"[1]

The master said, "Everyone is endowed with the wonderful."

1   See also no. 194.

282

A monk said, "I'm leaving for the south, and want to leave with a little knowledge about the Buddha-Dharma. What about it?"

The master said, "You are leaving for the south. If you come to a place where there is a Buddha, quickly move on. At a place where there is no Buddha, do not tarry."

The monk said, "In that case, I am dependent on nothing."

The master said, "Willow catkins, willow catkins."[1]

1   It was the custom in China, when saying goodbye to a friend who was going afar, to wave willow branches as the friend set off. The fuzzy willow catkins would fill the air and blow in the wind.

283

A monk asked, "What is that which is immediately at hand?"

The master said, "One question, one answer."

284

A monk asked, "The 'three inches'[1] is not depended upon, then is the present moment utilized or not?"

The master said, "I follow what you say, what do you make of it?"[2]

1   The tongue.
2   "What do you think, are you utilizing the present moment?"

285

A monk asked, "What is your 'family custom'?"

The master said, "In the vast boundlessness of time and space there are numberless people."

The monk said, "I asked, but you did not answer me."

The master said, "I have obviously done so."

286

A monk asked, "Two dragons are fighting for a pearl, which one gets it?"[1]

The master said, "The one that loses lacks nothing, the one that wins gains nothing."

1 See also no. 263.

287

A monk asked, "What is the form of a great man?"[1]

The master said, "What is this?"[2]

1 See no. 249.
2 Probably thrusting his own body forward at the same time.

288

A layperson came to present a robe to the master and asked, "To wear such a robe is wronging the people of the past, isn't it?"

The master threw down his whisk and said, "Is this past or present?"

289

A monk asked, "What is the practice of a sangha member?"

The master said, "Showing a hand, but not showing a foot."[1]

1 Not saying everything.

290

A monk asked, "What about when Nui-t'ou (Gozu) had not yet seen the Fourth Patriarch?"[1]

The master said, "Enough firewood, enough water."

The monk said, "What about after he saw him?"

The master said, "Enough firewood, enough water."

1   See no. 83.

291

A monk asked, "What is my self?"
  The master said, "Have you eaten breakfast or not?"
  The monk said, "I have eaten."
  The master said, "Then wash out your bowls."

292

A monk asked, "What is the teacher of Vairocana?"
  The master said, "Have you brought a white camel with you or not?"
  The monk said, "I've brought one."
  The master said, "Take him and feed him some grass."

293

A monk asked, "What is 'untutored wisdom'?"[1]
  The master said, "I have never taught you."

1   The wisdom that everyone has naturally from the time they are born.

294

A monk asked, "What is one pertinent statement?"
  The master said, "You've talked it to death."[1]

1   See also no. 172.

295

A monk asked, "If I do not use my mouth, may I have a discussion with you or not?"

The master said, "Obviously it is time."

The monk said, "Please discuss."

The master said, "I haven't brought anything up."

296

A monk asked, "The Second Patriarch cut off his arm, what sort of act is that?"

The master said, "He was throwing his whole self into it."[1]

The monk said, "To whom was the offering made?"

The master said, "The offering was made to whoever came."

1 A colloquial saying; literally the words mean "smashing the bones, breaking the body".

297

A monk asked, "Why wasn't Wu-pien-shen (Muhenmi) Bodhisattva able to see the halo of the Tathagata?"[1]

The master said, "You are a monk."

1 In the *Nirvana Sutra* the Tathagata (Shakyamuni Buddha) was expounding the sutra and Wu-pien-shen Bodhisattva was one of the bodhisattvas in the congregation. Wu-pien-shen means "boundless body".

298

A monk said, "In the day there is sunlight, at night there is firelight. What is 'divine light'?"

The master said, "Sunlight, firelight."

299

A monk asked, "What is the perfect question?'

The master said, "[That's] wrong!"

The monk said, "What is 'not asking'?"
The master said, "Consider what I just said."

300

A monk asked, "What is the form of a great man?'
The master cleaned off his face, straightened himself up, and sat
with his hands folded on his chest.

301

A monk asked, "What is non-action?"
The master said, "That [asking a question] is action."[1]

1   The opposite of non-action; action with a purpose.

302

A monk asked, "What is the mind that the Patriarch brought from
the west?"
The master said, "Inside the pen the ox is forgotten about."[1]

1   When you have put the ox in the pen, you no longer think about it. You are
    assured of its whereabouts.

303

A monk asked, "I have come a long way, please instruct me."
The master said, "You have only just entered my door. Is it
proper that I spit in your face?"

304

A monk asked, "What is the one road that 'cuts right through'?"[1]
The master said, "Has the boat from Wai-nan[2] arrived yet?"
The monk said, "I don't know."

The master said, "Good, it has arrived."

1 The one road that cuts right through ignorance and confusion.
2 A river in the south of Honan province, quite far from Chao-chou's (Joshu's) place.

305

A monk asked, "Does the oak tree have Buddha-nature or not?"
The master said, "It does."
The monk said, "When will it become Buddha?"
The master said, "When the sky falls to the ground."
The monk said, "When will the sky fall to the ground?"
The master said, "When the oak tree becomes Buddha."

306

A monk asked, "What is the mind that was brought from the west?"
The master said, "Why are you swearing at me inside the temple?"
The monk said, "What transgression have I made?"
The master said, "I don't swear at you while I am in the temple."

307

A monk asked, "What is the mind that was brought from the west?"
The master said, "Mould is growing on your teeth."

308

A monk asked, "This poor man[1] has come. How can he be saved?"
The master said, "You are not poor."
The monk said, "Then how do you deal with the fact that I am begging from you?"
The master said, "By just firmly staying poor."[2]

1   The monk is referring to himself.
2   By being steadfast in poverty.

309

A monk asked, "Why couldn't Wu-pien-shen (Muhenmi) Bod-hisattva see the halo of the Tathagata?"[1]

The master said, "It was like removing a transparent piece of silk."

1   See no. 297.

310

A monk asked, "Who is able to partake of the sweet dew of all the Heavenly worlds?"

The master said, "Thanks for bringing them."

311

A monk asked, "What about a person who has gone beyond Creative and Receptive?"[1]

The master said, "I'm waiting for there to be such a person to reply to him."

1   Heaven and Earth: the two polarities of the universe as presented in the Taoist *I Ching*.

312

A monk asked, "What is the sangha?"

The master said, "Entrance gate, Buddha hall."[1]

1   Two buildings of a Ch'an (Zen) temple. "Sangha" refers not only to the people who are in it, but to the place where they live.

313

A monk asked, "What is the 'unborn and undying'?"

The master said, "From the beginning unborn, right now undying."

314

A monk asked, "What is the master of Chao-chou (Joshu)?"[1]

The master said, "The king."

1 See also nos. 29, 36.

315

A monk asked, "I ask you to say something about that which is immediately at hand."[1]

The master said, "Pissing is an easy matter, I can do it by myself."

1 See also no. 283.

316

A monk asked, "What is a sixteen-foot golden Buddha?"[1]

The master said, "The shoulders are joined to the neck."

The monk said, "I don't understand."

The master said, "If you don't understand, go ask somebody to settle the matter."

1 See no. 77.

317

A monk asked, "What about when I have a doubt?"

The master said, "Is it 'great concordance' or 'small concordance'?"[1]

The monk said, "Great doubt."

The master said, " 'Great concordance' is the north-east corner; 'small concordance' is behind the monk's hall."[2]

1   The word for "doubt" and the word for "concordance" are homonyms in Chinese. Chao-chou (Joshu) is playing with the monk's words yet by the nature of his first answer the monk cannot understand that he is doing so.

2   The answer is using the ideas of building divination whereby buildings have a harmony with the local environment as part of the universe.

318

A monk asked, "What is a person that goes beyond Buddha?"

The master came down from his seat, looked the monk up and down and said, "This fellow is just this tall, he can probably be cut into three pieces. What 'upper' and 'lower' are you asking about?"[1]

1   The words for "above" and "below" are the same as those for "goes beyond" and "lesser than". Chao-chou (Joshu) is again freely playing with the monk's words.

319

A nun asked, "What is the deeply secret mind?"

The master squeezed her hand.

The nun said, "Do you still have that in you?"[1]

The master said, "It is you who have it."

1   "Are you still attached to that?"

320

The master instructed the assembly saying, "Thirty years ago, when I was in the south, I was the monk in charge of the fires and I had a conversation without host and guest.[1] To this very day no one had said anything."

1   Without subject and object.

321

A monk asked, "Having received the offerings of the king such as you have, what will you bring him in return?"

The master said, "*Nien-fu (Nembutsu)*!"[1]

The monk said, "I am a poor man but I can do 'nien-fu'."

The master said, "Call the attendant and get a penny from him."

1   The practice of invoking the name of the Buddha.

322

A monk asked, "What is your 'family custom'?"

The master said, "Even though the partition screen is down, its framework is still intact."

323

A monk asked, "What is the changeless principle?"

The master said, "You tell me; those wild ducks over there, have they flown here from the east or from the west?"

324

A monk asked, "What is the mind that the Patriarch brought from the west?"

The master said, "From where have you brought this information?"

325

The monk asked, "What is a 'person amidst the dusts'?"[1]

The master said, "Give me some money for tea and salt please."[2]

1   A person who lives in the world.

2 When monks begged for money it was called "getting money for tea and salt",
   i.e. everyday needs.

326

A monk asked, "T'a-erh San-tsang (Daiji Sanzo) tried to find the
National Teacher three times but couldn't see him.[1] It's not clear to
me, where was the National Teacher?"

The master said, "In San-tsang's nose."

1 T'a-erh San-tsang was a monk who had come from India and was proficient
   in the three classes of scripture (*San-tsang*) and reputed to have the power to
   read minds. Though he went to visit Nan-yang Hui-chung (Nanyo Echu), the
   National Teacher, he couldn't penetrate his mind.

327

A monk asked, "What about when the blind turtle happens on the
floating plank?"[1]

The master said, "It's not an accident."

1 In the *Saddharma Pundarika Sutra* there is a story about a sea turtle whose
   only eye is on its stomach and longs to see the sun. One time he happens upon
   a floating plank with a hole in it, and he manages to get a look at the sun
   through it by manoeuvring his body. It is a metaphor for the great difficulty
   of meeting with the Buddha-Dharma.

328

A monk asked, "What about when I've lived in mountains and
caves for a long time?"

The master said, "Why didn't you stay out there?"

329

A monk asked, "What is the great essence of the Buddha-Dharma?"

The master said, "Make your bow."[1]

While the monk was trying to say something further, the master called to his attendant Wen-yuan (Bun'en)[2] to come forward.

The master said, "Where were you a moment ago?"[3]

1   After the interview with the Ch'an (Zen) master a monk always bowed.
2   See Biography.
3   Wen-yuan's action is straightforward and unhesitating.

330

A monk asked, "What is the original mind of my own family?"
The master said, "I will not use the ox cleaver."[1]

1   In the analects of Confucius there is a saying that an ox cleaver is not used to carve a small fowl.

331

A monk asked, "For a long time I've heard about the famous stone bridge of Chao-chou (Joshu), but coming here I saw only a common wooden bridge."[1]

The master said, "You saw only the wooden bridge, you have not seen the stone bridge of Chao-chou."

The monk said, "What is the stone bridge of Chao-chou?"

The master said, "Cross over! Cross over!"

1   In those days a stone bridge was an uncommon thing. However, the monk is using the stone bridge as a metaphor of Chao-chou's Ch'an (Zen).

332

Another time a monk asked, "For a long time I've heard about the famous stone bridge of Chao-chou (Joshu), but coming here I saw only a common wooden bridge."

The master said, "You saw only the wooden bridge, you have not seen the stone bridge of Chao-chou."

The monk said, "What is the stone bridge of Chao-chou?"

The master said, "Horses cross, donkeys cross."

333

A monk asked, "What is your family name?"

The master said, "In Ch'ang-chou (Joshu)."[1]

The monk said, "How old are you?"

The master said, "In Su-chou (Soshu)."

1   Ch'ang-chou and Su-chou are two areas of China. Chao-chou's meaning is that there are lots of people with the same family name as me in Ch'ang-chou, and there are lots of old men in Su-chou.

334

The master entered the hall and said, "'Even if you have good and bad only a little, in the confusion mind is lost.'[1] Does anyone have something to say to that?"

A monk came forward and struck the attendant, saying, "Why don't you reply to the master?"

The master returned to his room.

Afterwards the attendant asked for elucidation and said, "Did that monk understand or not?"

The master said, "Those sitting see those standing; those standing see those sitting."

1   From the *Treatise on Being True to Mind* (*Hsin-hsin ming*).

335

A monk asked, "What is the Way?"[1]

The master said, "It's just outside the fence."[2]

The monk said, "I'm not asking about that."

The master said, "What 'way' are you asking about?"

The monk said, "The Great Way."

The master said, "The great way leads to the capital."

1   The word "way" also means "road", and the "great way" also means highway.
2   "You can't miss it."

336

A monk asked, "What about it when the dust is wiped away and the Buddha is seen?"

The master said, "It is not that the dust has not been wiped away, but that the Buddha is impossible to see."

337

A monk asked, "What is the body of no disease?"
The master said, "The four elements, the five attributes."[1]

1   The four elements are earth, fire, wind and water. The five attributes are matter, perception, consciousness, action and knowledge. These were commonly held as the constituents of the human anatomy.

338

A monk asked, "What is an icchantika?"[1]
The master said, "Why don't you ask about *bodhi*?"[2]
The monk said, "What is bodhi?"
The master said, "Just that is being an icchantika."

1   See no. 193.
2   Transcendental Wisdom.

339

The master made a fist and said, "I call this a fist. All of you, what do you call it?"

A monk said, "Why do you instruct us by means of objectivity?"

The master said, "I am not instructing you by objectivity. If I were to instruct you by means of the objective world, I would have entirely done away with you."

The master then said, "How will you deal with this?" and took his leave.

340

A monk asked, "One question, one answer is to fall completely into the heresies of Heaven and Hell. Even if there is silence, the rights of the other person are still violated. What is Chao-chou's (Joshu's) 'family custom'?"

The master said, "You don't know what you're asking about."

The monk said, "'Please answer."

The master said, "If it depended upon you,[1] you'd certainly get twenty blows."

1   "If the expression of my 'family custom' in regard to this depended upon you ..."

341

The master instructed the assembly saying, "'Even if you have good and bad only a little, in the confusion mind is lost.'[1] Do you have anything to say about this or not?"

A monk came forward, struck the attendant, and left.

The master returned to his room.

The next day he asked the attendant, "That monk yesterday, where is he now?"

The master said, "At that time he left."

The master said, "After thirty years of riding the best horses, I have given the whip to a donkey."

1   From the *Treatise on Being True to Mind* (*Hsin-hsin ming*). See also no. 334.

342

A monk asked, "If a person comes to you, as I have, do you teach him or not?"

The master said, "I teach him."

The monk said, "If a person does not come to you, do you teach him?"

The master said, "I teach him."

The monk said, "I grant that you teach the one who comes to you, but how do you teach one who does not come to you?"

The master said, "Stop! Stop! You mustn't talk about it. 'My Dharma is subtle and hard to think about.'"[1]

1   These words are borrowed from the *Saddharma Pundarika Sutra*. See also no. 202.

343

The King of Chen asked, "You are quite aged, how many teeth do you have left?"

The master said, "I have but one tooth."

The King said, "How do you manage to eat?"

The master said, "Even though there's but one, I chew one bite at a time."

344

A monk asked, "What is my pearl?"[1]

The master said, "Ask louder, please."

The monk bowed.

The master said, "You don't know what you're asking about. Why don't you say, 'I'm not asking about loud and quiet. What is my pearl?' Why don't you ask like that?"

The monk then asked his question again.

The master said, "I almost let this fool get by."

1   "Pearl" is a metaphor for "True Self".

A monk asked, "Both sides[1] are completely at rest. How do you explain this?"

The master said, "This year has been without eventful changes."

1   The two sides of duality (form and emptiness) are not discriminated, yet exist.

A monk asked, "The whole assembly has gathered, surely you will say something to us?"

The master said, "Today, drag a tree over here and build the monks' hall with it."

The monk said, "This is your instruction to us, isn't it?"

The master said, "I don't know anything about backgammon or long journey."[1]

1   These were parlour games common in T'ang China.

A monk asked, "What is the substance of the true person?"

The master said, "Spring, summer, autumn, winter."

The monk said, "In that case, it is hard for me to understand."

The master said, "You asked about the substance of the true person, didn't you?"

A monk asked, "What is the great spirit of the Buddha-Dharma?"

The master said, "What's your name?"

The monk said, "Me."

The master said, "Inside the Han-yuan Hall, within the Chin-yung Garden."[1]

1   The Han-yuan (Gangen) Hall was the name of the imperial palace in Chang-

an (Choan). The Chin-yung (Kinkon) Garden is a famous stone garden near Lo-yang (Rakuyo). Chao-chou (Joshu) is using these as metaphors for the basic reality of the universe.

349

A monk asked, "What is the teacher of the seven Buddhas?"[1]

The master said, "Sleeping when it's time to sleep, waking when it's time to wake."

1 The "seven Buddhas" are the seven historical Buddhas, of which Shakyamuni is the seventh.

350

A monk asked, " 'The Way is not outside of things, the outside of things is not the Way.' What is the Way that is outside of things?"

The master struck him.

The monk said, "Don't hit me or afterwards I will be someone who was wrongly beaten."

The master said, "Though it's easy to distinguish dragon and snakes, it's difficult to deceive a good monk."[1]

1 This conversation is probably an error in the text as in both the *Records of the Transmission of the Lamp* and the *Collections from the Halls of the Patriarchs*, it is rendered as taking place between Nan-ch'uan (nansen) and Chao-chou (Joshu).

351

The master, upon seeing the king come into the temple, did not rise. The master slapped his knee with his hand and said, "Do you understand?"

The king said, "No, I don't."

The master said, "I left home when I was a young man and now I'm old. I no longer have the strength to leave my seat to meet people."

352

A monk asked, "What are honest words?"

The master said, "Your mother is ugly."

353

A monk asked, "What is a person who doesn't forget anything of the past and present?"

The master said, "You should not try to tie down the mind. Be mindful of the Buddha everywhere in all things."

354

A monk asked, "What are honest words?"

The master said, "Eat an iron stick!"

355

A monk asked, "What is the fact that goes beyond Buddha?"[1]

The master clapped his hands and laughed.

1   See also no. 225.

356

A monk asked, "From one candle, hundreds and thousands of candles are lit. It's not clear to me, from where has the one candle come?"

The master kicked off one of his shoes and said, "A good person does not ask about such things."

357

A monk asked, "'By returning to the root the essence is attained, by following forms the foundation is lost."¹ What about it?"

The master said, "I have nothing to say about those words."

The monk said, "Please answer."

The master said, "It is obviously so."

1   From the *Treatise on Being True to Mind* (*Hsin-hsin ming*).

358

A monk asked, "What is the state of 'no-thought'?"

The master said, "Speak quickly! Speak quickly!"

359

A monk asked, "'Night rises in the Tsusita Heaven, day descends in the land of Jambu.'¹ Why doesn't the Mani Jewel² appear there?"

The master said, "What did you say?"

The monk repeated his question.

The master said, "Vipasyin Buddha³ immediately set his mind to it, but even until this day he has not attained its subtlety."

1   The reference is to a writing by Wu-chu (Mujaku, 310–390) that when night rises in the Tsusita Heaven (where the future Buddha Maitreya lives), future generations instantly receive Maitreya's teachings, and so day descends in the land of Jambu (the world).

2   The Mani Jewel is a perfect jewel that reflects all colours without itself having any colour, the jewel of perfect freedom.

3   Vipasyin Buddha was the first of the historical Buddhas.

360

A monk asked, "What is the state where there are no layers of thought?"

The master said, "Speak quickly! Speak quickly!"

A monk asked, "What is 'the treasure in the lining of the robe'?"[1]
The master said, "What do you dislike about that question?"
The monk said, "That is the question, but what is the treasure?"
The master said, "In that case, the robe has been forgotten."

1   In the *Saddharma Pundarika Sutra* there is a story about a rich traveller who
gets drunk and becomes worried about his treasure. So he sews it into the
lining of his robe to prevent it being lost or stolen. When he awakes from his
drunken stupor, he forgets what he has done and is forced to lead the life of
a beggar until such time as he remembers what he did. It is a metaphor for our
own Buddha-nature that we do not recognize.

362

A monk asked, "What about when there is no place to put up at
ten thousand miles?"[1]
The master said, "Stay at a Ch'an (Zen) temple."

1   There is no objectivity established. The dimension of emptiness. The character literally means "store", "shop", or "inn", a place to stop at.

363

A monk asked, "Does a dog have Buddha-nature or not?"
The master said, "The door of every house leads to the capital
(Chan-an)."

364

A monk asked, "Right before your eyes I am completely manifest.
Then is great mind realized in this or not?"
The master said, "Don't talk so loudly."
The monk said, "What about the state where there are no
restraints?"[1]

The master said, "I said, 'Don't talk so loudly'."

1   No restraints on the "great mind".

365

A monk asked, "What is the statement that is right before your eyes?"[1]

The master said, "I'm not as good as you."[2]

1   The monk is referring to himself.
2   "I'm not one statement."

366

A monk asked, "To have come here, what kind of people are we?"

The master said, "Buddhas and bodhisattvas."

367

A monk asked, "What about it when the mystical herb has not yet sprouted?"[1]

The master said, "If their fragrance is smelled, your brains will fall out."

The monk said, "What about it when their fragrance is not smelled?"

The master said, "It's as if you're dead on your feet."

The monk said, "Then do you acknowledge my oneness?"

The master said, "When someone comes, don't say anything to him."[2]

1   See also no. 215. The metaphor is of the world of undifferentiated unity.
2   "How can I tell you? How can you tell someone else?"

368

A monk asked, "Is the mind of the Patriarchs and the mind of the scriptures the same or different?"

The master said, "Someone who has just 'left home', but has not yet received the commandments, is whom you should ask about this."[1]

1 This is a question that any beginner in Ch'an (Zen) can answer.

369

A monk asked, "What is holy?"

The master said, "Not ordinary."

The monk said, "What is ordinary?"

The master said, "Not holy."

The monk said, "What about when there is neither ordinary nor holy?"

The master said, "That's a good Ch'an (Zen) monk."

370

A monk asked, "Two mirrors are facing each other.[1] Which is the clearest?'

The master said, "Your eyelids hang over Mount Sumeru."[2]

1 "You and I are facing each other."
2 In Buddhist cosmology, Mount Sumeru is the centre of the universe.

371

A monk asked, "I have just recently entered the assembly. I beg for your instruction."

The master said, "Good Heavens!"

372

A monk asked, "What about when the first word has been stated but the last word has not yet been uttered?"

The master said, "It won't do to call it anything."

The monk said, "Please define it."

The master said, "Ask me [about it]."

373

A monk asked, "What about when it is difficult to make the climb up the highest pinnacle?"

The master said, "I'm not on a high peak."

374

A monk asked, "What sort of a person is someone who has no connection with the ten thousand dharmas?"

The master said, "Not a person."

375

A commissioner asked, "Please say a word about the essence of the Buddhist tradition."

The master said, "Today I have no money to give to you."[1]

1   The commissioner was probably a tax collector.

376

A monk asked, "I don't have a special question. Please don't give a special reply."

The master said, "How extraordinary."

377

A monk asked, "Outside the teachings of the three vehicles,[1] how do you teach people?"

The master said, "Since this world came into being, the Sun and

Moon have never been replaced."[2]

1 Traditional Buddhism.
2 "How do the Sun and Moon teach you?"

378

A monk asked, "There is no intercourse with the three realms, how is knowledge to be left behind?"[1]

The master said, "Knowledge is beyond you."[2]

1 The three realms are senses, emotions and intellect.
2 "You're thinking about 'leaving it behind' but you can never leave it behind."

379

A monk asked, "All different kinds of workings have come together.[1] It's not clear to me, what is the fact that is 'there'?"[2]

The master said, "My eyes have always been quite good so I don't talk about the fact that is 'there'."

1 The interpenetrating circumstances that constitute the present.
2 See no. 278. These words have special stress on this that is here and now.

380

A monk asked, "What sort of person is it that does not stop in the Pure Land?"[1]

The master said, "You're not a person who is 'there'."

The monk said, "What is a person who is 'there'?"

The master said, "Stopped!"

1 A person who does not rest content with their own enlightenment but works to help other people have the same experience does not "stop at the Pure Land".

A monk asked, "What is the origin of the ten thousand dharmas?"
The master said, "Ridgepole, rafters, joists, pillars."
The monk said, "I don't understand."
The master said, "You don't understand standing at attention with folded hands."[1]

1 During a conversation with the master, monks stood at attention with their hands folded on their chests. The monk was doing that when Chao-chou (Joshu) said this.

382

A monk asked, "What about it when I don't have anything?"
The master said, "Throw it away."[1]

1 In the *Compendium of the Five Lamps* (*Wu-teng Hui-yuan*; *Goto Egen*) the questioner was Yen-yang Tsun-su (Ganyo Sonshuku), who was one of the heirs of Chao-chou (Joshu). In the *Compendium* it is recorded that he goes on to say, "I do not have anything, what is there to throw away?" Chao-chou (Joshu) then said, "In that case, take it away with you." At these words Yen-yang was enlightened.

383

A monk asked, "'When meeting a person of attainment on the road, greet him with neither words nor silence.'[1] It's not clear to me, how do you greet him?"
The master said, "From a person who comes from Ch'en-chou, you cannot get news about Hsu-chou."[2]

1 This is from the poem *T'an-tao ko* (*Tandoka*) by the Ch'an (Zen) master Hsiang-yen Chih-hsien (Kyogen Chikan).
2 Ch'en-chou and Hsu-chou are two different areas of China.

384

A monk asked, "Opening the mouth is doing something, what is doing nothing?"

The master pointed to his hand and said, "This is doing nothing."

The monk said, "That is doing something, what is doing nothing?"

The master said, "Doing nothing."

The monk said, "That is doing something."

The master said, "It is doing something."

385

The master instructed the assembly saying, "I don't like to hear the word 'Buddha'."

386

A monk asked, "Do you help people or not?"

The master said, "Buddha! Buddha!"

387

A monk asked, "Completely doing away with the world, what is it that clearly stands out?"

The master said, "If the world has been completely done away with, don't ask about it."

The monk said, "What stands out?"

The master said, "I said, 'don't ask'."

The monk said, "How can it be seen?"

The master said, "Its greatness has no outside; its smallness has no inside."

A monk asked, "What about when the four statements are left behind and the one hundred negations are gone beyond?"[1]

The master said, "I cannot know about death."

The monk said, "That is the fact of your own nature."[2]

The master said, "Maybe so."

The monk said, "Please instruct me."

The master said, "If the four statements are left behind and the one hundred negations are gone beyond, what instruction is there?"

1 See no. 9.
2 See also no. 12.

A monk asked, "What is your 'family custom'?"

The master said, "Having nothing inside, seeking for nothing outside."

A monk asked, "What is 'By returning to the root the essence is attained'?"[1]

The master said, "To answer [you] is to deviate."

1 From the *Treatise on Being True to Mind* (*Hsin-hsin ming*). See also no. 357.

A monk asked, "What is a 'doubting mind'?"[1]

The master said, "To answer [you] is to deviate."

1 The word "doubt" could be a copyist's error for the word "seek". Thus, the question could be "What is seeking for the mind?"

392

A monk asked, "Does a man who has left home become a house-holder or not?"

The master said, "To 'leave home' is to be a monk; but I don't pay attention to either 'leaving home' or 'not leaving home'."

The monk said, "Why don't you pay attention?"

The master said, "To do so is to leave home."[1]

1 "When I don't pay attention to 'leaving' or 'not leaving' it is to 'leave'."

393

A monk asked, "What about when there is neither master nor disciple?"

The master said, "The 'uncontaminated wisdom nature' is possessed from the beginning."

Later he said, "This is being without master and disciple."

394

A monk asked, "What about when 'external form is disregarded'?"[1]

The master said, "Why do you want to do that?"

1 See also no. 164.

395

A monk asked, "Clear yet not pure, muddy yet not turbid – what about this?"

The master said, "Not pure, not turbid."

The monk said, "What is that?"

The master said, "What a pity."

The monk said, "What is 'travelling through the world'?"

The master said, "Leaving 'diamond Ch'an'!"[1]

1 See no. 112.

396

A monk asked, "What is 'the treasure in the lining of the robe'?"[1]

The master said, "What do you dislike?"

The monk said, "What about when the action is not thorough-going?"

The master said, "Do you put a value on your own family?"

Later the master said, "If you act, it is is expensive; if you do not act, it is cheap."

1 See no. 361.

397

A monk asked, "What is the Patriarch's clear and obvious mind?"

The master drooled [as if he were sick].

The monk said, "What is the fact of 'there'?"[1]

The master spat on the ground.

1 These words are stressing "this right here and now". See also no. 379.

398

A monk asked, "What is the practice of a sangha member?"

The master said, "Leaving practice behind."

399

A monk asked, "Please point out the state of 'true ease'."

The master said, "Pointing it out makes it uneasy."

400

A monk asked, "What about when I have no questions?"

The master said, "You deviate from everyday talk."

401

A monk asked, "What about when the four mountains close in on each other?"[1]

The master said, "There are no signs of escape."[2]

1 The "four mountains" could be either the mountains of the four directions or birth, old age, sickness and death. See also no. 227.
2 "Though I escape, there are no signs of escape."

402

A monk asked, "What about it when upon arriving 'here'[1] nothing can be said?"

The master said, "Nothing can be said."

The monk said, "What shall I call it?'

The master said, "That about which nothing can be said."

1 "Here" is the counterpart of "there" and indicates the realm of enlightenment.

403

A monk asked, "All possible verbal expressions completely fail to go beyond limits [of one's own thinking]. What is the fact that is beyond limits?"

The master called to his attendant Wen-yuan (Bun'en).

Wen-yuan answered, "Yes?"

The master said, "What time is it?"

404

A monk asked, "What is the teacher of Vairocana?"[1]

The master said, "Don't use profanity."

1 See nos. 268, 292.

405

A monk asked, "'There's nothing difficult about the True Way, just refrain from picking and choosing.'¹ What is 'not picking and choosing'?"

The master said, " 'In Heaven above and Earth below, I alone am honoured.'"²

The monk said, "That is still 'picking and choosing'."

The master said, "You stupid oaf! Where is the 'picking and choosing' in it?"

1 From the *Treatise on Being True to Mind* (*Hsin-hsin ming*). See also no. 32.
2 The words said to have been spoken by Shakyamuni Buddha when he was born. See also no. 157.

406

A monk asked, "What is a person who is outside the three worlds?"¹

The master said, "But I am inside the three worlds."²

1 The three worlds are the world of desire, the world of form, the world of no form.
2 "So how can I know?"

407

A monk asked, "What about a person who is aware of 'is' and 'is not'?"¹

The master said, "If you ask again you will be purposefully questioning me."

1 "Is" and "is not" are two of the four statements. See no. 9.

408

The master instructed the assembly saying, "Don't stay here, get yourselves to the 'forests'¹ in the south."

A monk asked, "What kind of place is it where you are?"
The master said, "Where I am there is brushwood."[2]

1   "Forests" are Ch'an monasteries which the monks of the monastery referred
    to as the "Ch'an forest".
2   In contrast to the forest.

409

A monk asked, "What is the teacher of Vairocana?"
The master said, "Reality is a disciple."[1]

1   This answer is not clear and there is a good chance that there is an error in
    the text at this point. Professor Akitsuki suggests it may read, "You are a dis-
    ciple".

410

A monk asked, "What about when 'By returning to the root the
essence is attained'?"
    The master said, "That's being very hasty."
    The monk said, "Thank you."
    The master said, "Where does that 'thank you' come from?"[1]

1   See also no. 192.

411

Lin Hsiang-k'ung (Ryu Shoko)[1] came to the temple, saw the master
sweeping the ground and asked, "You are an accomplished person,[2]
why are you sweeping the dusts?"
    The master said, "They've come from the outside."[3]

1   A minor official.
2   The double meaning is that a master does not discriminate between dirty and
    clean or that a master does not do such menial work.
3   "You've brought them (in) with you."

412

A monk asked, "What about when the sharp sword is drawn from its scabbard?'

The master said, "Black."

The monk said, "I have asked straightforwardly, how do you discern 'white'?"

The master said, "I don't have any time to waste [on that]."

The monk said, "How do you deal with the man with folded hands who is in front of you?"[1]

The master said, "As soon as I see your folded hands."

The monk said, "What about it when there are no folded hands?"

The master said, "Who is it that has no folded hands?"

1   The monk is referring to himself.

413

A monk asked, "Where can a sangha member be of service?"

The master said, "Where can you not be of service?"

414

A monk asked, "What is the place that you instruct your disciples about?"

The master said, "There is no disciple in front of me."

The monk said, "In that case, you have not come out into the world."

The master took his leave.

415

A monk asked, "Is the mind of the Patriarch and the mind of the scriptures the same or different?"

The master made a fist and put it on his head.

The monk said, "Do you still have that?"[1]

The master took his cap off and said, "What is it that you have to say to me?"

1   "Do you still have that artifice of teaching?"

416

A monk asked, "What about it when the mind neither stops nor moves on?"

The master said, "It's alive! But [saying] that is obviously making use of it with the intellect."

The monk asked, "How can you not make use of it with the intellect?"

The master bowed his head.

417

A monk asked, "From what is the Way born?"

The master said, "That[1] would be being born, but the Way is not subject to birth and death."

The monk said, "Isn't that nature?"

The master said, "That[1] is nature, however the Way is not so."

1   What you say.

418

A monk asked, "Are the mind of the Patriarch and the mind of the scriptures the same or different?"

The master said, "If you can understand the mind of the Patriarchs, you will understand the mind of the scriptures."

419

A monk asked, "What is the action of difference in sameness?"

The master said, "*An-pu-lin-fa* (*An-bu-rin-patsu*)!"[1]

1   A tantric mantra. See no. 98.

420

A monk asked, "What about when the high pinnacle is difficult to climb?"

The master said, "I myself am on the mountain."

The monk said, "How do you deal with the steepness of Ts'ao-ch'i (Sokei) road?"[1]

The master said, "Ts'ao-ch'i's road is no good."[2]

The monk said, "Why is it that no one arrives there these days?"

The master said, "Because it is a high pinnacle."

1   The Sixth Patriarch, Hui-neng (Eno).
2   His road is not a six-lane paved freeway.

421

A monk asked, "What is the precious moon in the sky?"[1]

The master said, "My ears are all clogged up."[2]

1   The monk is asking about enlightenment.
2   "Why are you asking such a stupid question?"

422

A monk asked, "What about when there is a 'hair's breadth of dif-ferentiation'?"[1]

The master said, "Course."

The monk said, "What about when the situation is responded to?"

The master said, "Bending."

1   See also no. 183.

423

A monk asked, "What is the practice of a sangha member?"

The master brushed off his clothes.

424

A monk asked, "What about that which is continuous between the Buddhas and Patriarchs?"[1]

The master said, "No one knows about it."[2]

1 See also no. 234.
2 "No one can tell you about it."

425

A monk asked, "It's not clear to me, what is a 'temporary expediency'[1] to be called?"

The master said "A 'temporary expediency'."

1 A teaching device to help people experience enlightenment.

426

A monk asked, "I have recently entered the forest[1] and have no understanding. I beg for your teaching."

The master said, "You have entered the forest. Any more than this is not understanding."

1 The monastery.

427

A monk asked, "How have the ancient worthies of the past instructed men?"

The master said, "If it was not for your question, I would not know about the ancient worthies."

The monk said, "Please instruct me."

The master said, "I'm not an ancient worthy."

428

A monk asked, "The Buddha flower[1] has not yet opened, how can True Reality be discerned?"

The master said, "Is that true or real?"[2]

The monk said, "The fact of whose nature is it?"

The master said, "I have a nature, you have a nature."

1   Enlightenment.
2   "Is what you say 'true' or 'real'?"

429

A monk asked, "What is Buddha?"

The master said, "Who are you?"

430

A monk asked, "What about it when the road is directly ahead?"

The master said, "The road is directly ahead."

431

A monk asked, "What is the unending depth of the Deep?"[1]

The master said, "Your questioning me is the unending depth."

1   This is the same as the "depth of the Deep", see nos. 38, 41 and 46.

432

A monk said, "When the satori flower has not yet opened, how can True Reality be discerned?"

The master said, "It is opened."

The monk said, "It's not clear to me, is it[1] 'true' or is it 'real'?"
The master said, "True is real, real is true."

1 "Is True Reality 'true' or 'real'?" The monk is playing a little game.

433

A monk asked, "Is there anyone who is not requiting the four kindnesses in the three worlds?"[1]
The master said, "There is."
The monk said, "Who is it?"
The master said, "You ungrateful and immoral fool!"

1 See no. 59.

434

A monk asked, "A poor man has come,[1] what will you give him?"
The master said, "You are not lacking."

1 The monk is referring to himself.

435

A monk asked, "What is the true master of Chao-chou (Joshu)?"
The master said, "I am Ts'ung-shen."[1]

1 Chao-chou's personal name.

436

An old woman asked, "I have a body with the five hindrances.[1] How can I escape them?"
The master said, "Pray that all people are born in Heaven and pray that you yourself drown eternally in a sea of hardships."

1 A person with five hindrances cannot become Buddha, nor four types of King of Heaven. A woman's body was supposed to have these "five hindrances".

437

A monk asked, "What about it when the clear moon is in the sky?"

The master said, "You're still a person of categories."[1]

The monk said, "Please lead me out of categories."

The master said, "When the moon has set, come and see me."

1   "You still think of enlightenment in terms of a 'stage' of being."

438

Once the master instructed the assembly saying, "When I went to Yueh-shan's (Yakusan's)[1] place there was only one thing said. Yet, from then until now, my stomach has stayed full."

1   See no. 209.

PART THREE

Poems & Records from Pilgrimages

439

Once, while the master was in his room doing meditation, the head monk came to him and said, "The king has come to pay respects."

After the king had paid homage and left, one of his attendants asked, "The king came here, why didn't you rise?"

The master said, "You don't understand. Where I am, when a man of low standing comes I meet him at the gate. When a man of middle standing comes I leave my seat to greet him. When a man of superior standing comes I greet him without leaving my seat. How could I say that the king is a man of middle or low standing? I am chary of slighting the king."

The king was pleased [to hear this] and gave offerings as thanks to the master three times.

440

The master once asked Chou Yuan-wai (Shu Ingai),[1] "Have you ever seen Lin-chi (Rinzai)[2] in one of your dreams or not?"

Chou raised his fist.

The master said, "What side are you looking at?"

Chou said, "I'm looking at this side."

The master said, "Where do you see Lin-chi?"

Chou was silent.

The master said, "Where have you come from?"

Chou said, "I neither come nor go."

The master said, "Though not an old crow, it has flown here and flies away."

1   Though there is no information about Chou Yuan-wai, Professor Akitsuki suggests he was a lay disciple of Lin-chi. "Yuan-wai" is an official title of a lesser official.

2   Lin-chi I-hsuan (Rinzai Gigen, d. 866) was the great Patriarch of the Lin-chi (Rinzai) sect of Ch'an. He lived in a neighbouring province of Joshu, and was undoubtedly well known to Chao-chou (Joshu). Lin-chi was a disciple of Huan-po Hsi-yuh (Obaku Kiun).

441

The master instructed the assembly saying, "'If even a little there is good and bad, in the confusion mind is lost'.[1] Then do you have anything to say in reply to this or not?"

Afterwards there was a monk who brought this up to Lo-p'u (Rakuho)[2]. Lo-p'u clacked his teeth [in reply].

Later the monk brought it up to Yun-chu (Ungo)[3]. Yun-chu said, "What need is there to reply?"

The monk reported these things to the master.

The master said, "In the south there are many men who destroy their bodies and give up their lives."

The monk said, "Please explain."

The master started to explain but the monk pointed to another monk who was standing nearby and said, "That monk has already eaten his fill, how will you speak to him?"

The master desisted [in his explanation].

1   From the *Treatise on Being True to Mind* (*Hsin-hsin ming*).

2   Lo-p'u Yuan-an (Rakuho Genan, 834–898) was a disciple of Chia-shan Shan-hui (Kassan Zenne). He lived in Li-chou (Rei-shu) in Hunan.

3   Yun-chu Tao-ying (Ungo Doyo, d. 902) was a disciple of Tung-shan Liang-

chien (Tozan Ryokai). He was one of the main masters in the Ts'ao-tung (Soto) sect of Ch'an and lived in Hung-chou (Koshu) in Kiangsi.

442

Once while the master was reading the *Vajracchedika Sutra* a monk asked, "'All the Buddhas and the Perfect Wisdom of all the Buddhas can all be attained from this sutra.'[1] What is this sutra?"

The master said, "'Diamond *Prajna-paramita Sutra*. Thus I have heard. Once the Buddha was in Sravasti ...'"[2]

The monk said, "That's not right."

The master said, "I can't amend the scriptures on my own."

1 The monk is quoting the *Vajracchedika Sutra*.
2 Chao-chou (Joshu) is reading from the sutra.

443

Once when a monk was leaving, the master said, "You're leaving. If someone asks you, 'Have you seen Chao-chou (Joshu) or not?', how will you reply to him?"

The monk said, "I will just say, 'I met him'."

The master said, "I am a donkey. How do you meet me?"

The monk had no answer.

444

The master asked a newcomer, "Where have you come from?"

The monk said, "From the south."

The master said, "Well, are you aware that there is a barrier of Chao-chou (Joshu)?"

The monk said, "Are you aware that there are those who don't cross the barrier?"

The master said, "You salt peddler!"[1]

Later he said, "Brothers, the barrier of Chao-chou is hard to pass through."

Someone said, "What is the 'barrier of Chao-chou'?"

The master said, "The stone bridge."

1 See also no. 272.

445

There was a monk who had come from Hsueh-feng's (Seppo's)[1] place.

The master said, "Don't stay at this place. Where I am is only a place where we keep out of the way of difficulties. The Buddha-Dharma is entirely in the south."

The monk said, "How can there be north and south in the Buddha-Dharma?"

The master said, "Even though you have just come from Hsueh-feng and Yun-chu (Ungo),[2] you are still only a 'pole carrier'."[3]

The monk said, "It is not clear to me, what about the affairs down there?"[4]

The master said, "How come you wet your bed at night?"[5]

The monk said, "What about after there is penetration?"[6]

The master said, "It's still a pile of shit."[7]

1 See Biography.
2 See no. 441.
3 Coolies carried poles on their shoulders. Chao-chou (Joshu) could be saying, "You're no better than anyone else", or he could be saying that the monk's understanding is one-sided, as Akitsuki suggests.
4 "What is your criticism of the Buddhism in the south?"
5 Chao-chou is deriding the monk's Ch'an (Zen) as not thoroughgoing.
6 After there is enlightenment.
7 "Your enlightenment would still be nothing special."

446

The master instructed the assembly, "At my place there is a lion that comes out of the cave, and a lion that stays in the cave. Yet, it's difficult to have a cub."

At that time a monk snapped his fingers as a reply.

The master said, "What's that?"

The monk said, "A cub."

The master said, "If I say it's a cub, there is immediately transgression. Can you then make another leap?"

447

The master asked a new arrival, "Where have you come from?"

The monk said, "From Hsueh-feng's (Seppo's) place."

The master said, "What has Hsueh-feng been saying as instruction to people?"

The monk said, "He always says, 'Throughout the whole wide world there are one-eyed sangha members. All of you, where is it that you take a shit?'"

The master said, "If you should go back there, take this trowel[1] with you."

1   The trowel was used to dig a hole and cover the faeces while travelling.

448

While the master was giving away material [to make robes] to the assembly, a monk asked, "You have completely given everything away, what will you use?"

The master said, "Man of Hu-chou!"[1]

The monk said, "Yes?"

The master said, "What are you using?"

1   The monk was evidently from Hu-chou, a town on the east coast of China.

449

The master instructed the assembly saying, "When the world was not, this reality was. When the world is destroyed, this reality is not destroyed."[1]

The monk asked, "What is this reality?"

The master said, "Five attributes, four elements."[2]

The monk said, "Those can still be destroyed."

The master said, "Four elements, five attributes."

1 See also no. 209.
2 See no. 337.

450

There was a priest from Ting-chou (Joshu) who came to visit.

The master asked him, "What practice do you undertake?"

The priest said, "Without listening to scriptures, commandments, or discourses, I understand them."

The master raised his hand and pointed to it saying, "Well, do you understand that?"

The priest was flustered and didn't know what to do.

The master said, "Even though you understand without listening, you are just a person who understands scriptures and disclosures. When it comes to the Buddha-Dharma, you don't know anything about it."

The priest said, "Your talking right now. Isn't it the Buddha-Dharma?"

The master said, "Even though you can ask and answer questions, these are still things of the scriptures and discourses. It is not yet the Buddha-Dharma."

The priest had no reply.

451

The master asked a traveller, "Where have you come from?"

The traveller said, "From a temple in the north."

The master said, "How is that temple similar to this one?"

The traveller could make no reply. There was a monk who was standing nearby and the master directed him to answer for the traveller.

The monk said, "I've come from that temple."

The master laughed.

The master then directed Wen-yuan (Bun'en)[1] to answer for the traveller.

Wen-yuan said, "I have not yet had words with you."

1   See Biography.

452

The master asked a priest, "What practice have you been doing?"

The priest said, "Trying to understand the *Vimalakirti-nirdesa Sutra*."

The master said, "In that sutra it is said, 'The practice hall is at every step'.[1] Where are you at?"

The priest couldn't answer.

The master directed Ch'uan-i (Zeneki)[2] to answer.

Ch'uan-i said, "Can't the practice hall be seen in that question?"

The master said, "Your body is the practice hall. Where is your mind? Try to say something."

Ch'uan-i said, "You are trying to seek out my mind."

The master said, "That's right."

Ch'uan-i said, "Just these questions and answers; what are they?"

The master said, "I am not doing anything intentionally, yet I am aware of the Dharma that goes beyond eyes, ears, nose, tongue, body and mind."

Ch'uan-i said, "If you are not doing anything intentionally, why are you seeking [for something]?"

The master said, "Because you were not able to say anything."

Ch'uan-i said, "The Dharma goes beyond eye, ear, nose, tongue, body and mind, yet is not realized. Why can't anything be said about it?"

The master said, "Eat my saliva."

1   See also no. 214.
2   Ch'uan-i is a disciple of Chao-chou (Joshu) about whom nothing else is
    known.

453

The master asked a monk, "Have you studied the *Saddharma Pun-darika Sutra*?"

The monk said, "I have."

The master said, "In that sutra it says, 'To wear the robe and live in a quiet place is given the name *aranya*.[1] The people of the world are deceived by it.' What do you make of it?"

The monk bowed.

The master said, "Can you put on that robe or not?"

The monk said, "It's on."

The master said, "Don't deceive me."

The monk said, "How can I not deceive you?"

The master said, "I can take care of myself, don't play with my words."

1   An Indian Sanskrit word for the quiet forest where the life of religious disci-
    pline is followed.

454

The master asked a priest, "What practice are you doing?"

The priest said, "Learning the *Vimalikirti-nirdesa Sutra*."

The master said, "Who is the author of that sutra?"

The priest said, "I am."

The master said, "Why then did you transmit it to your descendants?'

The priest could not reply.

455

One day the master entered the hall and a monk started to come forward to ask a question. The master immediately bowed and retired.

Another time a monk came to ask a question and the master said, "Well done. Ask a question."

The monk asked, "What is Ch'an (Zen)?"

The master said, "Today is overcast, I can't reply."

456

The master asked a new arrival, "Where have you come from?"

The monk said, "From no direction."

The master turned his back on the monk.

The monk picked up his bowing cloth and turned around like the master.

The master said, "That's a fine 'no direction'."

457

The master asked a new arrival, "Where have you come from?"

The monk said, "From the south."

The master said, "Having met outside the three thousand miles,[1] don't play with me."

The monk said, "I don't understand."

The master said, "Take up willow branches, take up willow branches."[2]

1 Outside the world.
2 Holding willow branches to watch the catkins blow in the wind was a game played by children in China. See also no. 282.

458

Feng-kuan (Bukan)[1] came to the foot of Mount Wu-t'ai (Godai)[2] and met an old man.

Feng-kuan said, "Aren't you Manjushri?"

The old man said, "There cannot be two Manjushris."

Feng-kuan bowed and the old man disappeared.

There was a monk who brought this up to the master.

The master said, "Feng-kuan had only one eye."

The master then told Wen-yuan (Bun'en) to act as the old man, and he himself would act as Feng-kuan.

The master said, "Manjushri, Manjushri."

1   Feng-kuan was the head priest at Kuo-ch'ing ssu (Kokusei-ji) where Han-shan and Shih-te (Kanzan and Jittoju) lived.

2   Mount Wu-t'ai was sacred to the bodhisattva of wisdom, Manjushri.

459

The master questioned two new arrivals.

The master asked the first one, "Have you been here before?"

The monk said, "No, I haven't."

The master said, "Go have some tea."

The master then asked the other monk, "Have you been here before?"

The monk said, "Yes, I have."

The master said, "Go have some tea."

The monk asked, "Setting aside the fact that you told the one who'd never been here before to go have some tea, why did you tell the one who had been here before to go have some tea?"

The master said, "Head monk!"

The head monk said, "Yes?"

The master said, "Go have some tea."

460

The master arrived[1] at Yun-chu's (Ungo's)[2] place.

Yun-chu said, "You who are so old, why haven't you found some place to stay?"

The master said, "Where is there to stay?"

Yun-chu said, "Right in front of you are the remains of an old temple."

The master said, "In that case, live there yourself."

1   The anecdotes that begin in this way occurred during the time when Chao-chu (Joshu) was on his pilgrimages after the death of his master Nan-ch'uan (Nansen).

2   See no. 441.

461

The master arrived at Shuyu's (Shuyu's)[1] place.

Shuyu said, "You are so old, why haven't you found some place to stay?"

The master said, "Where is there to stay?"

Shuyu said, "You who are so old do not know the place to stay."

The master said, "For thirty years I've ridden the best horses, yet today I must give the whip to an ass."

1   Shuyu was a descendent of Nan-ch'uan (Nansen); hence he was a brother monk of Chao-chou (Joshu). He lived in Go-chou (Gaku-shu) in modern Hupei.

462

The master later went to Shuyu's room and looked it over.

Shuyu said, "You're losing your balance on flat ground.[1] What for?"

The master said, "It's just because my mind is so barbaric."[2]

1   Shuyu is disparaging Chao-chou's (Joshu's) impoliteness.

2   "I'm not so refined and well mannered as you."

463

One day the master went into the main hall at Shuyu's temple holding a staff, and walked around from east to west.

Shuyu said, "What are you doing?"

The master said, "Looking for water."

Shuyu said, "I haven't a drop here, what are you looking for?'

The master leaned the staff against a wall and left.

464

On the road to Mount Wu-t'ai (Godai) there was an old woman who always conversed with the monks who came there.

A monk would ask, "Which way is it to the Wu-t'ai road?"

The old woman would say, "Go straight on."

As the monk set off she would say, "There goes another one like that."

The master heard of this and went to question her.

As the master set off, the old woman said, "There goes another one like that."

The master then returned [to the temple] and told the assembly about what had happened and said, "Today I thoroughly saw through the old woman."

465

The master saw a monk coming and held up a burning stick. Pointing to the stick the master said, "Do you understand?"

The monk said, "No."

The master said, "You can't call it 'fire'. That's all I have to say about it."

Again the master held up the burning stick and said, "Do you understand?"

The monk said, "No."

The master said, "From here, go to Shu-chu (Joshu) where

T'ou-tzu (Tosu)[1] lives. Go visit him and ask him about this. If the circumstances for you are right, you needn't come back here.[2] If they are not right, come back here again."

The monk left and when he came to T'ou-tzu's place, T'ou-tzu asked him, "Where have you come from?"

The monk said, "I've left Chao-chou (Joshu) especially to come here."

T'ou-tzu said, "What has Chao-chou been saying?"

The monk then told of what happened.

T'ou-tzu got up from his seat, took a few steps, sat down and said, "Do you understand?"

The monk said, "No."

T'ou-tzu said, "Go back and tell Chao-chou about this."

The monk then came back to Chao-chou and told the master what happened.

The master said, "Do you understand?"

The monk said, "Not yet."

The master said, "There's no difference."[3]

1 T'ou-tzu T'a-t'ung (Tosu Daido, 819–914) was a disciple of Ts'ui-cheng (Suibi). He was one of the great Ch'an (Zen) masters of the time and a close friend of Chao-chou's. His temple was in Shu-chou which was about four hundred miles from Chao-chou's temple.

2 "If you find that you can understand the Dharma better at T'ou-tzu's place, stay there."

3 "There's no difference between T'ou-tzu and myself."

466

Tung-shan (Tozan)[1] asked a monk, "Where have you come from?"

The monk said, "From making sandals."

Tung-shan said, "Have you done it by yourself or with the aid of others?"

The monk said, "With the aid of others."

Tung-shan said, "Have the others then instructed you or not?"

The monk made no reply.

The master answered for him[2] and said, "With your permission, it is just as you say."

1   Tung-shan Liang-chieh (Tozan Ryokai, 807–869) was the famous founder of the Ts'ao-tung (Soto) sect of Ch'an (Zen). He was the disciple of Yun-yen (Ungan).

2   At a later date most likely.

467

P'u-hua (Fuke)[1] was eating lunch[2] and, upon seeing him, Lin-chi (Rinzai)[3] said, "P'u-hua is an ass!"

P'u-hua then brayed like an ass.

Lin-chi said nothing more.

P'u-hua said, "That bastard Lin-chi has only one eye."

The master later said, "He was simply offering [Lin-chi] the fodder of his own nature."[4]

1   P'u-hua was an eccentric priest and a good friend of Lin-chi's. He was the successor of P'an-shan (Banzan). Though little is known of his life, he is revered as the founder of the P'u-hua (Fuke) sect of Ch'an (Zen) whose practice is the playing of the bamboo flute (shakuhachi).

2   P'u-hua was eating at Lin-chi's temple as he had no temple of his own.

3   See no. 440.

4   Paying Lin-chi back for the lunch in his own way.

468

Pao-shou (Hoju)[1] asked Hu-ting-chiao (Koteiko),[2] "Aren't you Hu-ting-chiao?"

Hu-ting-chiao said, "You're too kind."

Pao-shou said, "Can you nail up the sky or not?"

Hu-ting-chiao said, "Please try to nail up the sky."

Pao-shou slapped him and said, "After this some jabbering scholar will explain this for you."

Hu-ting-chiao told the master about this.

The master said, "Why did you make him hit you?"

Hu-ting-chiao said, "I don't know what my error was."

The master said, "There's but one seam, so what is to be done about it? You should go again and have him hit you."

Hu-ting-chiao understood the point.

The master said, "Just nail up one seam."

1 Pao-shou was one of the major successors of Lin-chi. He lived in Chen-chou (Chin-shu) to the north of Chao-chou (Joshu).

2 Hu-ting-chiao was a lay person. His name means "loose hinge nail".

469

Once, while the master was walking in the road, he met an old woman who asked him, "Where do you live?"

The master said, "To the west of the East Temple in Chao-chou (Joshu)."

The master told this to his monks and said, "You tell me, what word did I use for 'west'?"[1]

One monk said, "The 'west' of east and west."

Another monk said, "The character for 'dwelling'."

The master said, "Both of you are wholly qualified to be officials in the salt or iron offices."[2]

1 This doesn't come across well in English, but in Chinese the word for 'west' is Hsi, for which there are many homonyms. The words that the monks suggest are both Hsi in Chinese.

2 "You both really know the language well."

470

The master and an official were wallking in the garden and saw a rabbit run away.

The official said, "You are a great and accomplished person, why did the rabbit run away when it saw you?"

The master said, "I like to kill."

Once the master saw a monk sweeping and said, "You are sweeping like this; then have you made things clean or not?"

The monk said, "The more it's swept, the more it needs to be swept."

The master said, "How can there be no one who is expelling the dust?"

The monk said, "Who is the person who expels the dust?"

The master said, "Do you understand?"

The monk said, "No."

The master said, "Go ask Yun-chu (Ungo)[1] about this."

The monk then went and asked Yun-chu, "What is the person who expels the dust?"

Yun-chu said, "He is a blind fool."

1 See no. 441.

The master asked a monk, "How long have you been here?"

The monk said, "Seventy-eight years."

The master said, "Then have you met me?"

The monk said, "I have met you."

The master said, "I am a donkey. How can you meet me?"

The monk said, "Entering into the Dharma world, I meet you."

The master said, "As I thought, you have only one side. You have eaten up much of our rice uselessly."

The monk said, "Please speak."

The master said, "Why didn't you say, 'I meet you when I look into the feed bin'?"

The master asked the cook, "For today's meal, will it be raw vegetables or cooked vegetables?"

The cook held up a vegetable leaf.

The master said, "Those who know kindness are few; those who abuse kindness are many."[1]

1   Chao-chou (Joshu) is saying, "Though what you say is all right, why do you have to make an issue of it?"

474

There was a layman on his travels who came to offer incense at the temple.

The master asked a monk, "He is over there offering incense. We are here talking. Right now, is life going on over there?"

The monk said, "What are you?"[1]

The master said, "In that case, it is over there."

The monk said, "In that case, it was that way before."[2]

The master laughed.

1   Living or dead.
2   "When you asked me."

475

The master was returning from the king's palace when he saw a stone sutra pillar[1] with one part missing.

A monk asked, "Has that one part of the sutra pillar gone to Heaven or gone to Hell?"

The master said, "It has gone to neither Heaven nor Hell."

The monk said, "Where has it gone?"

The master said, "It has fallen over."

1   A "sutra pillar" was a pillar of six sides with words of a scripture written on it.

The master and his disciple Wen-yuan (Ban'en)[1] were having a discussion in which they were not supposed to come to a decisive conclusion. The one who made a conclusion would have to buy some bean cakes.

The master said, "I am an ass."

Wen-yuan said, "I am the harness of the ass."

The master said, "I am the faeces of the ass."

Wen-yuan said, "I am the bugs in the faeces."

The master said, "What are you doing in there?"

Wen-yuan said, "Passing the summer training period in there."

The master said, "Go buy some bean cakes."

1   See Biography.

477

While the master was sitting, a monk started to come forward to ask a question. The master said, "Thank you for your trouble."[1]

While the monk was trying to express his question the master said, "Still?"

1   These words were always said by the master when he had finished a discourse.

478

Once the master was standing on the porch and heard some swallows chirping.

The master said, "That chirp-chirping of the swallows is their [way of] talking to us people."

A monk asked, "It's not clear to me, are they doing it intentionally or not?"

The master said, "Faintly hearing the suggestion of a melody,/The wind is made to blow a different tune."[1]

1   From a poem by Kao-P'ien.

479

There was a monk who was taking leave.

The master said, "Where are you going?"

The monk said, "Fukien."

The master said, "There are a great many soldiers in Fukien. How will you avoid them?"

The monk said, "Where can I go to avoid them?"

The master said, "Well come!"[1]

1   See also no. 108.

480

A monk was on his way to interview the master, but he saw that the master was sitting with his robe covering his head, so he went back.

The master said, "You can't say I didn't answer you."

481

The master asked a monk, "Where have you come from?"

The monk said, "From the south."

The master said, "Who has been your companion?"

The monk said, "A water buffalo."

The master said, "You're a good monk, why did you make a beast your companion?"

The monk said, "Because there are no differences."[1]

The master said, "Forgetting that I don't approve, come and take me as a companion in place of the water buffalo."

1   "There's no difference between me and the water buffalo."

482

The master asked a monk, "Is the Patriarch[1] in this hall or not?"

A monk said, "He is here."

The master said, "Tell him to come and wash my feet for me."

1   The first Ch'an (Zen) Patriarch, Bodhidharma.

483

In the monks' hall there were two monks yielding to each other about who would sit in the first seat. One of the elder monks told the master about it.

The master said, "Both of them should sit in the second seat."

The monk said, "Who will sit in the first seat?"

The master said, "Light the incense."

The monk said, "It is lit."

The master said, "The fragrance of rules, the fragrance of meditation."[1]

1   Two of the five fragrances of the Dharmakaya.

484

The master asked a monk, "Where have you come from?"

The monk said, "From the capital."[1]

The master said, "Did you pass through the T'ung-kuan pass?"

The monk said, "I didn't go through there."

The master said, "Today I've caught a salt peddler."[2]

1   Lo-yang (Rakuyo).
2   See no. 272.

485

Once the master was "seeing off"[1] a dead monk and said, "There is but one dead man, yet he got numberless people to see him off."

Then he said, "How many dead men send off one living man?"

At that time a monk asked, "Is it mind that is born, or body that is born?"

The master said, "Mind and body are both unborn."

The monk said, "Then what about that thing?"[2]

The master said, "It's a dead man."

1   Attending a funeral.
2   The dead body.

486

There was a monk who saw a cat and asked, "I call that a cat. It is not clear to me, what do you call it?"

The master said, "It is you that calls it a cat."

487

Once the King of Chen came to visit and the master's attendant came to inform him of it.

The attendant said, "The king has come."

The master said, "How are you, Your Majesty?"

The monk said, "He's not here yet, he's at the temple gate."

The master said, "Yet you said, 'The king has come'."

488

Once, while the master was in the latrine, he called out to Wen-yuan (Ban'en).

Wen-yuan answered, "Yes?"

The master said, "I'm in the latrine now and needn't expound the Dharma any further for you."

489

Once, while passing through the king's palace, the master called to his attendant.

The attendant answered, "Yes?"

The master said, "Fine indeed is the skilfulness of the palace."[1]

The attendant made no reply.

1 Chao-chou (Joshu) is referring to the reply of the attendant.

490

Once the master arrived at Lin-chi's (Rinzai's)[1] place and began to wash his feet.

Lin-chi asked, "What is the mind that the Patriarch brought from the west?"

The master sad, "Right now, I'm washing my feet."

Lin-chi bent forward as if he had not heard the master's words.

The master said, "If you understand, then understand. If you don't understand, don't keep pecking over it. What will you do?"

Lin-chi brushed off his sleeves and left.

The master said, "I've been travelling for thirty years, and today I have heedlessly given an explanation to someone."[2]

1 See no. 440.
2 The account of this encounter given in the *Lin-chi lu-yu* (*Rinzai-roku*) puts Chao-chou (Joshu) and Lin-chi in roles opposite to those given here.

491

The master came to Kuo-ch'ing ssu (Kokusei-ji) on Mount T'ien-tai (Tendai), and met Han-shan and Shih-te (Kanzan and Jittoju).[1]

The master said, "For a long time I've been hearing about Han-shan and Shih-te, but having come here I just see two water buffalo."

Han-shan and Shih-te put their fingers on their heads like horns.

The master said, "Shoo! Shoo!"

Han-shan and Shih-te gnashed their teeth and glared at each other.

The master went back to the monks' hall; the two men followed him and asked, "What about the circumstances that happened[2] a moment ago?"

The master laughed heartily.

1   Han-shan and Shih-te are two of the most famous figures in the Ch'an (Zen) of the T'ang dynasty. They were poet hermits who lived at Kuo-ch'ing ssu and in the mountains that surround it.

2   *Innen* (*pratitya-samutpada*): inter-penetrating circumstances that are the basis of all phenomena.

492

Another day the two men asked the master, "Where have you come from?"

The master said, "From paying respects to five hundred hon-ourable priests."[1]

The two men said, "They're five hundred water buffalos, those honourable priests."

The master said, "Why are you making the five hundred hon-ourable priests into water buffalos?"

Han-shan said, "Good Heavens!"

The master laughed heartily.

1   Paying respects to the various Ch'an (Zen) masters.

493

When the master was on pilgrimage, he met two hermits. One of them appeared to be a young boy. The master gave greetings to them, but the two took pains not to look up. Early the next morn-ing the young boy brought one pot of rice, set it down on the ground, and divided it into three parts. The other hermit brought up his seat next to the pot and sat down. The young boy sat down across from him, but they did not call the master. The master brought up his own seat and sat down by the pot. The young boy looked straight into the master's face.

The hermit said, "It is not as if he got up early, but still there is a night traveller here."[1]

The master said, "Why don't you give this traveller instruction?"

The hermit said, "He is a member of my family."

The master said, "He's almost left entirely alone and free."[2]

The young boy then got up, looked at the hermit, and said, "Why are you such a chatter-box?" He then went into the mountains and disappeared.

1 This account shows examples of how the young boy, as the attendant of the hermit, was being impolite. What the hermit says is an oblique reference to the young boy and an apology to Chao-chou (Joshu).

2 Refers to the statement "He's a member of my family".

494

Once, while the master was reading a scripture, Wen-yuan (Ban'en) came into his room.

The master turned the scripture so that Wen-yuan could see it and pointed to it.

Wen-yuan left the room.

The master went after him, grabbed him, and said, "Speak quickly. Speak quickly!"

Wen-yuan said, "Amitabha Buddha! Amitabha Buddha!"[1]

The master went back to his room

1 See no. 269.

495

Once a young novice[1] came to interview the master.

The master said to his attendant, "Get him out of here."

The attendant said to the novice, "The master wants you to leave."

The novice bowed and left.

The master said, "That young novice has entered the gate,[2] you are still outside the gate."

1   A young boy who has not yet become a monk.
2   Entered the gate of the sangha, i.e. become a monk.

496

While the master was on pilgrimage, he came to the temple of a priest.

He had just entered the gate when they met each other and the master said, "Is there anything here? Is there anything here?"

The priest held up his fist.

The master said, "It's difficult to drop anchor in shallow waters."

Later he arrived at another temple, saw the priest, and said, "Is there anything here? Is there anything here?"

The priest held up his fist.

The master said, "You are able to give or take away, you are able to be casual or strict."

497

The master one day held a *juzu*[1] and asked a Korean priest, "Are there any of these where you come from or not?"

The priest said, "There are."

The master said, "Are they like this one?"

The priest said, "They are not like that one."

The master said, "There are some, so how are they not like this one?"

The priest couldn't answer.

The master himself answered, saying, "Can't you say, 'China, Korea'?"

1   A circular string of one hundred and eight beads, similar to a rosary, which Buddhist priests carry.

498

The master asked a new arrival, "Where have you come from?"

The monk said, "From the south."

The master raised a finger and said, "Do you understand?"

The monk said, "No."

The master said, "You don't even understand 'hello, how are you'."

499

When the master was on pilgrimage, he asked T'a-tzu (Daiji),[1] "In what way does *prajna*[2] function as 'substance'?"

T'a-tzu said, "In what way does prajna function as 'substance'?"

The master laughed heartily and left.

The next day T'a-tzu saw the master while he was sweeping and asked, "In what way does prajna function as 'substance'?"

The master let go of his broom, laughed heartily, and left.

T'a-tzu returned to his room.

1 T'a-tzu Huai-chung (Daiji Echu, 780–862) was the disciple of Po-chang (Hyakujo), and he lived in Hang-chou (Koshu).

2 An Indian Sanskrit word for "intuitive wisdom".

500

The master came to Po-chang's (Hyakujo's)[1] place.

Po-chang asked, "Where have you come from?"

The master said, "From Nan-ch'uan (Nansen)."

Po-chang said, "What has Nan-ch'uan been saying to instruct people?"

The master said, "One time he said, 'A man who as yet has no attainment should be strict and solemn'."

Po-chang scoffed at this.

The master appeared startled.

Po-chang said, "That's a fine 'strict and solemn'."

The master did a little dance and left.

1 Po-chang Huai-hai (Hyakujo Ekai, 720–814) was a disciple of Ma-tsu (Baso) and a brother monk of Nan-ch'uan (who was Chao-chou's teacher). His temple was in the north part of modern Kiangsi. He is one of the great Ch'an (Zen) masters esteemed as the founders of the Lin-chi (Rinzai) sect of Ch'an.

501

The master came to T'ou-tzu's (Tosu's)[1] place and was eating lunch with him.

T'ou-tzu took a bean cake and offered it to the master.

The master said, "No thanks."

T'ou-tzu immediately took down another bean cake from the shelf, and ordered the attendant to hand it over to the master.

The master accepted the cake and bowed three times to the attendant.

T'ou-tzu remained silent.

1 See no. 465.

502

Once a monk drew the master's portrait and showed it to the master.

The master said, "If I look like that, beat me to death. If I don't look like that, burn it."

503

Once, while the master was out walking with Wen-yuan (Ban'en), he pointed to a pile of earth and said, "That would be a good place for a patrol-box."

Wen-yuan then went over to the place, stood there, and said, "Give me your passport."[1]

The master punched him.

Wen-yuan said, "Your passport is in order. Pass on."

1   See no. 272.

504

The master asked a new arrival, "Where have you come from?"

The monk said, "Mount Wu-t'ai (Godai)."

The master said, "Then did you meet Manjushri or not?"

The monk held up his hand in the posture of Manjushri.

The master said, "You can hold up your hand many times, but who is it that sees Manjushri?"

The monk said, "Only those who get nervous."

The master said, "'Without seeing the wild geese in the clouds,/How can the cold of the northern frontier be known?'"[1]

1   There was an old saying that when the geese are seen heading south, you know the cold will be coming to the northern outposts in the Gobi Desert.

505

A monk asked, "I have come from afar to meet you. Please give me some instruction."

The master said, "In the school of Sun-pin (Sonbin) why did they drill holes in the tortoises?"[1]

The monk brushed off his sleeves and left.

The master said, "Although he was about to do something quite splendid, those two feet of his were cut off."

1   Sun-pin was a diviner in ancient China who had both his feet cut off as a punishment.

506

The master and the head monk went to see the stone bridge.[1]

The master asked, "Who built this?"

The head monk said, "Li-yen (Riyo)."

The master said, "When he was building it where did he lay his hands on it?"

The head monk couldn't answer.

The master said, "People are always talking about the stone bridge, yet when I ask about it they don't know where to lay their hands on it."

1   The famous stone bridge of Chao-chou.

507

There was a Korean priest who asked the master to come to lunch.

The master arrived at the front gate and asked, "What temple is this?"

The priest said, "A Korean temple."

The master said, "You and I are an ocean apart."

508

The master asked a monk, "Where have you come from?"

The monk said, "From Yun-chu (Ungo)."[1]

The master said, "What teaching has Yun-chu been giving lately?"

The monk said, "There was a monk who asked, 'What about it when the antelope hangs by its antlers?'[2] The master (Yun-chu) said, 'Six, six, three, ten, six'."

The master said, "Brother Yun-chu is still fine."

The monk said, "It's not clear to me, what is your thought about this?"

The master said, "Nine, nine, eight, ten, one."

1   See no. 441.
2   The antelope was thought to hang from tree limbs when it slept so that no tracks were left behind.

509

There was an old woman who came into the temple at nightfall.

The master said, "What are you doing?"

The old woman said, "I've come to stay overnight."

The master said, "What place is this place?"[1]

The old woman laughed heartily and left.

1   "Do you know where you are?"

510

The master went out [for a walk] and ran into an old woman who was carrying a basket.

The master asked, "Where are you going?"

The old woman said, "I'm taking bamboo shoots to Chao-chou (Joshu)."

The master said, "When you see Chao-chou what will you do?"

The old woman walked up and slapped the master.

511

Once the master saw the head monk giving the meal offering[1] to the birds, who all flew away upon seeing him.

The master said, "When the birds see you, why is it that they fly away?"

The head monk said, "They're afraid of me."

The master said, "What are you saying?"

The master himself answered and said, "It's because I have a killer's mind."[2]

1   The offering that each monk takes out of his food at each meal to offer to "hungry spirits".
2   See also no. 470.

The master asked a monk, "Where have you come from?"

The monk said, "From Kiangsi."

The master said, "Where do you find Chao-chou (Joshu)?"

The monk could not answer.

The master was leaving the main hall when he saw a monk bowing to him.

The master struck him with his stick.

The monk said, "But bowing is a good thing!"

The master said, "A good thing is not as good as nothing."

The master once came to T'ung-kuan pass. The guard at T'ung-kuan asked, "Do you know you are at T'ung-kuan pass?"

The master said, "I know it."

The guard said, "Those who have a passport can be let to pass; those who have no passport cannot be let to pass."

The master said, "What about it when the emperor's coach happens to come?"

The guard said, "It must still be checked to pass through."

The master said, "You want to start a revolution."

The master came to Pao-shou's (Hoju's)[1] place.

Pao-shou saw him coming and sat down with his back to the master.

The master spread out his bowing cloth.

Pao-shu stood up.

The master left.

1   See no. 468.

When the master was at Nan-ch'uan's (Nansen's), Nan-ch'uan led an ox into the monks' hall and walked around the hall with it. The head monk hit the ox three times on the back. Nan-ch'uan then stopped.

Afterwards, the master took a blade of grass in his mouth and stood in front of the head monk. The head monk couldn't answer.

517

There was a young official who, upon seeing the master, praised him saying, "You are an old Buddha."

The master said, "You are a young Tathagata."[1]

1 Tathagata is another name for Buddha.

518

There was a monk who asked, "What is nirvana?"
    The master said, "I didn't hear you."
    The monk repeated his question.
    The master said, "I'm not deaf."
    The master then recited a verse:

He who dances and skips on the Great Way,
Is face to face with the Nirvana Gate.
Just sitting with a boundless mind,
Next year spring is still spring.

519

There was a monk who asked, "Birth and death are two roads. Are they the same or different?"

The master had a verse that said:

A man of the Way asks about birth and death,
How can birth and death be discussed?
Water in the pond of the *sala* forest,[1]
The bright moon illuminates Heaven and Earth.
To speak to him of a consciousness beyond words
Is but playing with ghosts.
If you want to understand birth and death,
It is a crazy man's talk of his dream about spring.

1   A forest of fragrant sandalwood trees; an imaginary idyllic place.

520

There was a monk who asked, "It is said, that 'when the Buddhas have difficulties they hide themselves within the flames'. When you have difficulties, where do you hide yourself?"
    The master had a verse that said:

He says the Buddhas have difficulties,
I say he has the problem.
Just watch the way I avoid difficulties
Where is it that they are following after us?
"Yes" and "No" are not spoken,
Coming and going are not coming and going.
I have spoken about the Dharma of difficulty for you,
Now come and get to know me.

521

Upon seeing a pagoda being built there was a verse:

From the beginning is completion,
Why labour to pile up stones?
Images may be carved,
But they are far removed from me.[1]
If someone were to ask me [about it],

Finally [I would say], "Don't even draw up the plans."

1   "The image of me is not really me."

522

Whenever there were contrary opinions[1] brought to the master he had a verse that said:

South of Chao chou (Joshu), north of the stone bridge,
Maitreya lives in Kuan-yin yuan (Kannon-in).[2]
The Patriarch left behind one sandal,[3]
To this day it has not been found.

1   From other Ch'an masters that were different from his own.
2   Maitreya is the Buddha of the future.
3   The reference is to a famous story about the death of Bodhidharma. Bodhidharma was poisoned by jealous Buddhist priests and buried at a temple on Bear's Ear Mountain. However, not long after that he was seen at the Plain of Wild Onions by a Chinese official who was returning from India over the pilgrim route. When the official reached Bear's Ear Mountain and told his story the grave was opened. The casket was empty except for one straw sandal.

523

For the drum used for chanting[1] there was a verse:

Made by the genius of the four elements that have come together,
That it has a voice is wholly the greatness of the emptiness in its head.
Don't wonder about it not speaking to the populace,
It is only because its speech is not the same as ordinary chatter.[2]

1   The *mokugyo*.
2   There is a poetic metaphor here referring to the ordinary musical scale.

524

Upon seeing lotuses there was a verse:

How marvellous, the sparkling of snow embraced in the
sprouting root,[1]
I wonder when it was removed from the Western Heaven.[2]
How deep the mud is no one realizes,
When it comes out of the water they immediately know it is a
white lotus.

1 "Sprouting root" is a reference to both the lotus and the universe.
2 "Western Heaven" means both India and the Buddha land.

525

Song of the Twelve Hours of the Day.[1]

The cock crows. The first hour of the day.[2]
Aware of sadness, feeling down and out yet getting up.

There are neither underskirts nor undershirts,
Just something that looks a little like a robe.
Underwear with the waist out, work pants in tatters,
A head covered with thirty-five pounds of black grit.
In such a way, wishing to practise and help people,
Who knows that, on the contrary, it is being a nitwit.

Sun level with the ground. The second hour of the day.[3]
A broken-down temple in a deserted village – there's nothing
worth saying about it.

In the morning gruel there's not a grain of rice,
Idly facing the open window and its dirty cracks.
Only the sparrows chattering, no one to be friends with,
Sitting alone, now and then hearing fallen leaves hurry by.
Who said that to leave home is to cut off likes and dislikes?
If I think about it, before I know it there are tears moistening
my hanky.

Sun up. The third hour of the day.[4]
Purity is turning into compulsive passions.

The merit of doing something[5] is to get buried in the dirt,
The boundless domain has not yet been swept.
Often the brows are knit, seldom is the heart content,
It's hard to put up with the wizened old men of the east village.
Donations have never been brought here,
An untethered donkey eats the weeds in front of my hall.

Meal time. The fourth hour of the day.[6]
Aimlessly working to kindle a fire and gazing at it from all
sides.

Cakes and cookies ran out last year,
Thinking of them today and vacantly swallowing my saliva.
Seldom having things together, incessantly sighing,
Among the many people there are no good men.
Those who come here just ask to have a cup of tea,
Not getting any they go off spluttering in anger.

Mid-morning. The fifth hour of the day.[7]
Shaving my head, who would have guessed it would happen
like this?

Nothing in particular made me ask to be a country priest,
Outcast, hungry, and lonely, feeling like I could die.
Mr Chang and Mr Lee,[8]
Never have they borne the slightest bit of respect for me.
A while ago you happened to arrive at my gate,
But only asked to borrow some tea and some paper.

The sun in the south. The sixth hour of the day.[9]
For making the rounds to get rice and tea[10] there are no special
arrangements.

Having gone to the houses in the south, going to the houses in
the north,

Sure enough, all the way to the northern houses I'm given only excuses.
Bitter salt, soured barley,
A millet-rice paste mixed with chard.
This is only to be called "not being negligent of the offering",
The Tao-mind[11] of a priest has to be solidified.

Declining sun. The seventh hour of the day.[12]
Turning things around, not walking in the domain of light and shade.[13]

Once I heard, "One time eating to repletion and a hundred days of starvation are forgotten,"
Today my body is just this.
Not studying Ch'an (Zen), not discussing principles,
Spreading out these torn reeds and sleeping in the sun.
You can imagine beyond Tsushita Heaven,[14]
But it's not as good as this sun toasting my back.

Late afternoon. The eighth hour of the day.[15]
And there is someone burning incense and making bows.

Of these five old ladies, three have goitre,
The other two have faces black with wrinkles.
Linseed tea, it's so very rare,
The two Diamond Kings[16] needn't bother flexing their muscles.
I pray that next year, when the silk and barley are ripe,
Rahula-ji[17] will give me a word.

Sun down. The ninth hour of the day.[18]
Except for the deserted wilderness what is there to protect?

The greatness of a monk is to flow on without any special obligations,
A monk going from temple to temple has eternity.
Words that go beyond the pattern do not come through the mouth,

Aimlessly continuing where the sons of Shakyamuni left off.
A staff of rough bramble wood;
It's not just for mountain climbing but also to chase off dogs.

Golden darkness. The tenth hour of the day.[19]
Sitting alone in the darkness of a single empty room.

For ever unbroken by flickering candlelight,
The purity in front of me is pitch black.[20]
Not even hearing a bell[21] vacantly passing the day,
I hear only the noisy scurrying of old rats.
What more has to be done to have feelings?[22]
Whatever I think is a thought of *Paramita*.[23]

Bedtime. The eleventh hour of the day.[24]
The clear moon in front of the gate, to whom is it begrudged?

Going back inside, my only regret is that it's time to go to
sleep,
Besides the clothes on my back, what covers are needed?
Head monk Liu, ascetic Chang,
Talking of goodness with their lips, how wonderful!
No matter if my empty bag[25] is emptied out,
If you ask about it, you'd never understand all the reasons for
it.

Midnight. Twelfth hour of the day.[26]
This feeling,[27] how can it cease even for a moment?

Thinking of the people in the world who have left home,
It seems like I've been a temple priest for a long time now.
A dirt bed, a torn reed mat,
An old elm-block pillow without any padding.
To the Holy Image[28] not offering any Arabian incense[29]
In ashes hearing only the shitting of the ox.

1   The Chinese hour is equivalent to two western hours.
2   1am to 3am.

3   3am to 5am.
4   5am to 7am.
5   Motivated action having a goal or purpose.
6   7am to 9am.
7   9am to 11am.
8   These names are used like "Mr Smith" and "Mr Jones" to refer to everyone.
9   11am to 1pm.
10 Begging.
11 Literally "mind of the Way", refers to the mind of enlightenment.
12 1pm to 3pm.
13 "Light and shade" also means "time".
14 Tsushita Heaven is the abode of the Buddha of the future, Maitreya.
15 3pm to 5pm.
16 The "Diamond Kings" refer to the two demi-god kings who are the guardians of the Buddha-Dharma.
17 Rahula was one of the ten disciples of the Buddha Shakyamuni. He was especially adept in the esoteric teaching and in healing. The appellation "ji" after his name shows endearment.
18 5pm to 7pm.
19 7pm to 9pm.
20   Literally "like the lacquer of Chin-chou (Kinshu)".
21 Bells were rung to denote times of the day in towns and in temples.
22 The natural feelings that are inherent in being a human being.
23 *Paramita* here means to have crossed over to the dimension of enlightenment. Every thought is an "enlightened thought".
24 9pm to 11pm.
25 Refers to both a money bag and also, metaphorically, to the body. The "empty bag being emptied out" refers to death.
26 11pm to 1am.
27 The state of mind of enlightenment.
28 The statue of Buddha.
29 Arabian incense was the most expensive type.

End of the Recorded Sayings of Ch'an Master Chao-chou

Appendix

Verse for the master's portrait made by the King of Chao-chou (Joshu).

The moon of the Blue Gorge.
The face in a clear mirror.
My master, my teacher,
The realm of Chao-chou.

Two eulogies of priest Chao-chou (Joshu).[1]

The master leaves the waters of the Chai (Shi)[2] and kings and princes are moved.
The light of his mind seal lies hid in the confines of the yak tail.[3]
The mists of the blue sky obscure the moonlight of pine peak,
In the deep dark waves, the boat of men's salvation capsizes.
A candle is suddenly extinguished and the Papiyans[4] rejoice,
With both eyes seriously dimmed, friends of the Way are saddened.
No matter if someone has passed completely through the clouds,[5]
Whenever he sees the jug or the loom,[6] tears will flow.

The sun of Buddha inclines toward the west, the seal of the Patriarchs breaks,
A pearl sinks into crimson mud, the moon loses its shine.

Shadows spread over the small room[7] and the fireplace weeps,
Breezes stir in the meditation hall and the pines softly moan.
The one sandal suddenly came and its traces are left behind,[8]
In the five heavens, where can he be met again?
Disciples who have understood emptiness, transcend joy and sorrow.
Yet with flowing tears they face the snowy drapes.[9]

1   It is thought that these two verses were written by the King of Chao-chou (Joshu).
2   The river that passes through Chao-chou.
3   The wish given to the King by Chao-chou upon his death as a symbol of Dharma transmission.
4   Evil spirits that delude men.
5   Become enlightened.
6   Things left behind by Chao-chou.
7   The room where the master lives.
8   The reference is to Bodhidharma and to Chao-chou as his Dharma descendant. See no. 522.
9   The drapes around the coffin.

The resident priest of Hsi-hsien Ch'an-yuan (Seiken Zenji) on Mount Lu (Ro), a monk who has received the Dharma and the purple robe, Ch'eng-shih (Choshoku),[1] has carefully, and with repeated corrections, set this down.

1   Ch'eng-shih was a successor of Po-chang Tao-heng (Hyakujo Doko) in the third generation of the Fa-yen (Hogen) sect of Ch'an. Though his dates are unknown, it can be assumed he lived in the last half of the tenth century.

Glossary

bodhisattva. An enlightened person who chooses to stay in the world and help others rather than leaving the world to enjoy the state of nirvana.

Buddha. The enlightened one. Buddhahood is a state of direct experiencing of the true nature of things.

Buddhakaya. The Buddha "body" or nature which is of three kinds: Dharmakaya, Sambhogakaya and Nirmanakaya (see below).

Dharma. The absolute Truth which underlies all existence.

dharma. Each phenomenon is also a dharma in the sense of being an expression of the Dharma, the absolute Truth.

Dharmakhaya. One of the three aspects or "bodies" of the Buddhakaya or Buddha-nature. It is the universal and pure essence. The other two are the Nirmanakaya and the Sambhogakaya.

karma. The sum total of the effects of one's past actions.

Maitreya. The name used to refer to the Buddha of the future.

Manjushri. A Buddhist demi-god who embodies the wisdom of non-dualistic mind.

Nirmanakaya. One of the three aspects or "bodies" of the Buddhakaya or Buddha-nature; the apparent forms aspect, i.e. the material world of changing forms.

nirvana. The state of "emptiness" that follows the emptying of desires and therefore of suffering. A state of perfect freedom, purity and tranquillity.

prajna. Intuitive Wisdom.

Sambhogakaya. One of the three aspects or "bodies" of the Buddhakaya or Buddha-nature; the responsive aspect, i.e. the emotional/psychological experiences that arise from the interplay between the Dharmakaya and the Nirmanakaya (see above) and which create the fabric of cause and effect.

sangha. The community of Buddhist monks and nuns; those who have undertaken to pursue the Buddhist life and renounce all worldly ties.

Shakyamuni. Another name for Gautama Buddha, the historical Buddha. "Shakyamuni" is used a lot in Zen to refer to Gautama because it refers more to the human aspect, somewhat like referring to the Catholic Pope by his given name.

Vairocana. "The Great Illuminator Buddha" which is the pure and universal essence of the Buddha equated with the Dharmakaya.

Printed in the United States
by Baker & Taylor Publisher Services